electric bass guitar

the complete guide

by Laurence Canty

I've been playing bass with Radiohead since its inception. I'm into the space a bass can occupy between the drums and the harmonies of guitar and voice, and how the instrument can become part of the soul of the band.

After recording The Bends, I decided that I wanted to find out more about the instrument. I was lucky enough to have a series of lessons with Laurence, using his book Electric Bass Guitar.

The book helped me to understand the freedom that harmony and chord theory can give a bass player. It also helped reinforce and develop what I already knew about rhythm and technique. One of the book's many strengths is that it can be used by any player, at any level - it is a very clear, concise introduction to the instrument. It has been repeatedly useful to me over the years, across several tours and albums - in fact, the bass line on Airbag (the first track of OK Computer) was the result of a lesson on chord theory with Laurence.

I'm still using this supportive, challenging, and confidence-inspiring book for tuition and reference.

Colin Greenwood
Radiohead

Book designed and realised by Brucciani Design Ltd
Editing by Barrie Carson Turner
Music setting by Chris Francis, Cambridge Notation
Photographs of Matthew Canty by Miki Slingsby (London)
Printed by Pagefast Print and Publishing Ltd

Published by Promenade Music
www.ElectricBassGuitarBook.com
ISBN 978-0-9562916-0-8

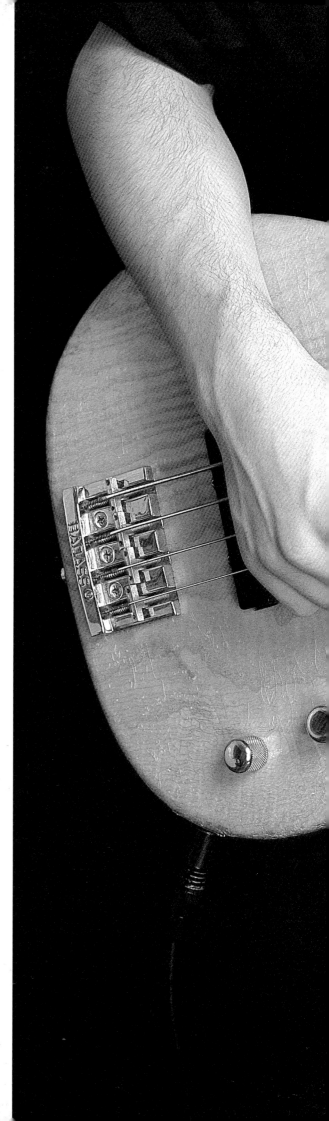

electric
bassguitar

the complete guide by Laurence Canty

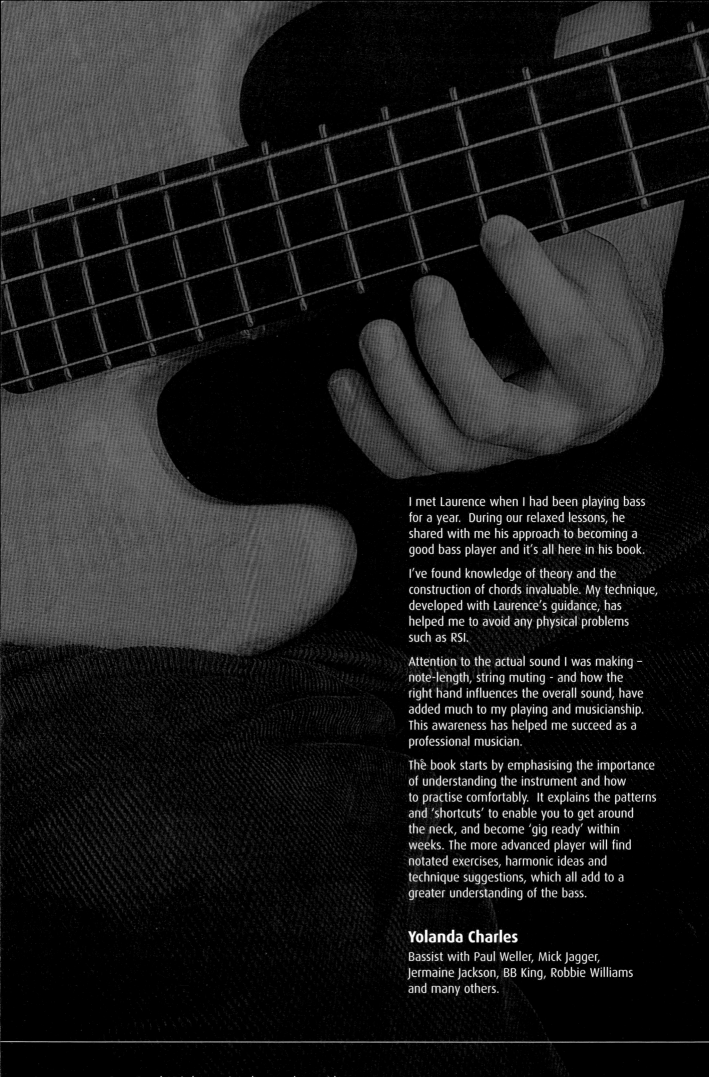

I met Laurence when I had been playing bass for a year. During our relaxed lessons, he shared with me his approach to becoming a good bass player and it's all here in his book.

I've found knowledge of theory and the construction of chords invaluable. My technique, developed with Laurence's guidance, has helped me to avoid any physical problems such as RSI.

Attention to the actual sound I was making – note-length, string muting - and how the right hand influences the overall sound, have added much to my playing and musicianship. This awareness has helped me succeed as a professional musician.

The book starts by emphasising the importance of understanding the instrument and how to practise comfortably. It explains the patterns and 'shortcuts' to enable you to get around the neck, and become 'gig ready' within weeks. The more advanced player will find notated exercises, harmonic ideas and technique suggestions, which all add to a greater understanding of the bass.

Yolanda Charles

Bassist with Paul Weller, Mick Jagger, Jermaine Jackson, BB King, Robbie Williams and many others.

1 machine head
2 head
3 nut
4 G-string
5 D-string
6 A-string
7 E-string
8 neck
9 fingerboard
10 fret
11 front pickup
12 back pickup
13 controls
14 jack socket
15 bridge
16 body

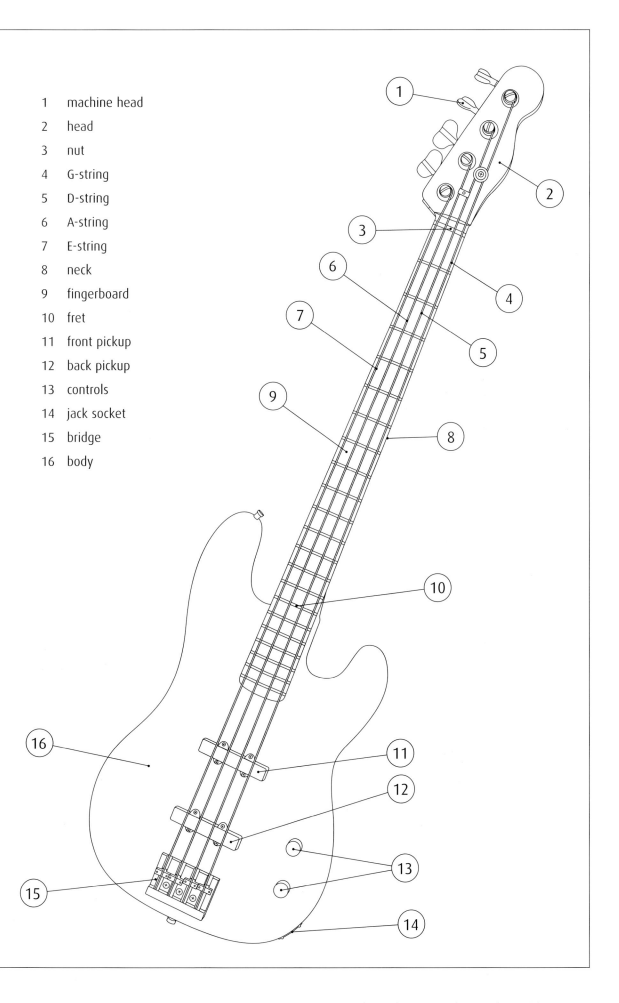

introduction

The first section of this book assumes nothing and covers the basics. At first an amplifier is not essential and your bass doesn't even have to be in tune. Once you've developed some technique and an understanding of the fingerboard you're ready to play. Initially play only the root of each chord. Provided you change to the next note at the right time there's no need to know about different types of chords or scales. Listen to the other musicians and fit in rhythmically.

The second section explains different chords and will enable you to add other notes to your bass lines. It includes exercises to develop technique, extend musical knowledge and train your ear. The phrase playing by ear is misleading because your ears can only check what your fingers have already done - so develop an awareness of what sound will be produced by a given fingering. To practise this, play exercises slowly and imagine the sound of the next note before you play it.

The third section develops an understanding of the links between chords and scales. This will help you to play from a chord chart, improvise, and extend your ideas. All this can be achieved without reading music - although it is there for those who can.

There are three areas that seem to cause confusion and difficulty - modes and minor scales, which are dealt with in the third section, and reading music, which is covered in the fourth. In each case the approach here is very different from elsewhere. For example, reading music intuitively by recognising familiar patterns rather than the usual counting approach. Learning to read music will help you practise more productively and explore new ideas more easily. Eventually you may develop the skill to sight-reading standard and be able to use it professionally.

There is no need to work through the book in sequence. While looking at the second or third section you could start on the fourth. Even the fifth section, covering advanced techniques, can be understood without reading music. Finally there's a selection of pieces by Bach that, although technically demanding, are easy to read - so you don't have to leave them until last. Probably it is better to study the various sections of the book in parallel.

The most important function of a bass player is to create effective bass lines. Inevitably you'll only play within your technical and musical limits. By extending these you will be able to produce better and more varied ideas - instantly if necessary.

Remember that a book can compress a lot of information in a few pages. Allow time to understand and absorb any new idea - until you can play it without thinking you don't really know it.

section one | basics

section two | scales and chords - basics

section three | scales and chords - advanced

section four | reading music

section five | more techniques

electric bass guitar | # section one

basics

technique

At first it will be easier to sit when you play. Choose a chair that does not restrict your arms and allows you to sit upright comfortably - a high stool is ideal. Rest the bass on your right leg. The position of the right arm places the fingers at the strings and balances the instrument. Now, keeping the left hand away from the neck, pick the D-string about 10cm from the bridge alternating the first and second fingers. After picking the string the finger must continue through and stop against the A-string to mute it. The thumb normally rests on the E-string for the same reason, so if your bass has a thumb rest now is the time to remove it. To produce a full tone use the weight of the whole finger to lean on the string as you pick it, rather than just flexing the fingertip.

To play with a pick use alternate up-strokes and down-strokes, making sure that there is no difference in tone between them. The pick should be held between the thumb and first finger - it is not necessary to exert great pressure to hold it.

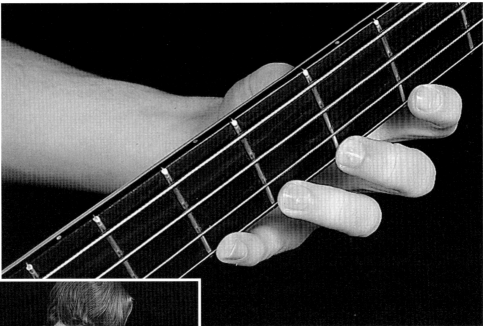

Now extend the fingers of your left hand and then place them on the G-string. At first keep the thumb away from the neck.

It may help to begin by placing the fourth finger on the string, followed by the third, second and first - with each finger as close as possible to each fret.

Lean the bass against you with the neck pointing up and away so that your left arm is relaxed, not pressed into your side and not resting on your leg.

Now place your thumb on the back of the neck - you should find that it is at the middle of the neck, approximately behind the second finger.

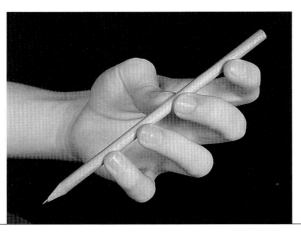

To check your hand position, hold a pen or pencil between your thumb and extended fingers. Notice how only slight pressure is required to achieve a comfortable balance.

When your first finger is on the SECOND fret you are in SECOND position. Initially this position may not be comfortable. If so, choose a higher one and then gradually move down until second position, and eventually first position, is possible. Adjusting the bass so that the neck is at a steeper angle will help extend your reach. This procedure needs to be repeated whenever you practise until you find that you can achieve a comfortable position immediately.

The position of the bass in relation to your body should be similar whether you are sitting or standing. When you stand and play, adjust the strap accordingly. It should support and balance the bass without any help from either hand.

Finally, before moving on to the next section, check that:

• The bass is balanced without any support from the left hand.

• The thumb is not exerting unnecessary pressure on the neck.

• The fingers are close to the frets so that least pressure is required.

• No part of the left hand, apart from the thumb and fingers, is in contact with the neck.

exercises

These exercises are designed to:

• Develop position playing - using one finger for each fret so that a four-fret range can be covered. Generally, it is better to use position playing since it reduces hand movement and so reduces effort. Variations on this basic technique will be explained later.

• Strengthen your fingers, especially the fourth, so that you can hold the strings down.

• Increase the control over your fingers - especially the third that has less independence.

• Develop the necessary finger spacing - especially separating the second and third correctly.

Pick the string once for each number. The double lines and dots at the end indicate that the whole sequence is repeated - in this case until you can play it confidently, with the notes even and the beat regular. The notation only shows which left-hand finger is used, so the exercises can be played in any position on the strings indicated. Initially aim for control, fluency and a regular beat rather than speed - which can be developed later. Start by playing only on the G-string and then gradually include the others.

STRING	G	D	A	E	A	D
FINGER	1 2 3 4	1 2 3 4	1 2 3 4	1 2 3 4	1 2 3 4	1 2 3 4 :

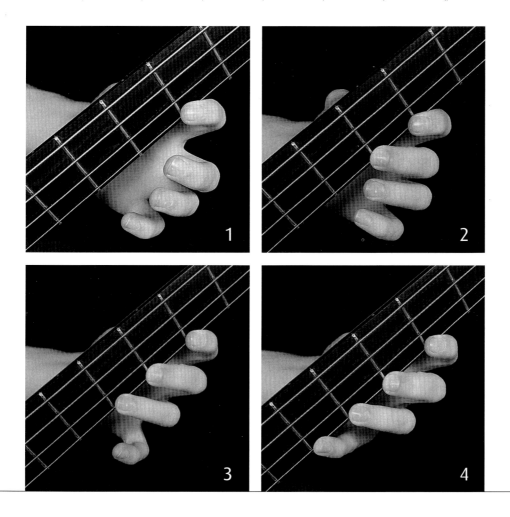

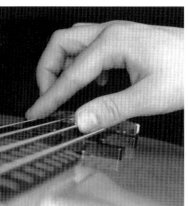

Some points to check while you're playing:

- Keep the rhythm consistent - no pauses when changing string and no slowing down on the lower strings. If possible use a drum machine.

- Sustain all notes by keeping the fingers down. This ensures that you are developing the required finger spacing.

- Keep the first finger flat across the strings as shown. This mutes the strings above the one being played.

- Use the hand position from the previous section with your fingers close to the frets. Develop a touch-awareness with your fingertips so that you can feel where the frets are.

- Only look at your fingers when you need to. Looking tends to make you think too much and that slows you down. Practise listening rather than looking and be aware of what both hands are doing.

- Check your technique using a mirror. It should look relaxed and effortless and not awkward or uncomfortable.

- Don't bend the strings - you may find that you tend to pull them, especially the A and E.

- Make sure that picking and fretting happen exactly together - if necessary play slowly to confirm this.

- Rest your right-hand thumb on the E-string except when you play:
  - the G-string
  Rest the thumb on the A-string so that it still touches the E-string and mutes both strings. The picking finger will mute the D-string.
  - the E-string
  Instead of resting the thumb on a pickup just lift it slightly off the string. It will then return to the E when you move to play another string.

- Pick the strings at different places and listen to how the tone changes. Near the bridge it's hard and bright but towards the neck it's round and deep. This is another reason for resting the thumb on the E-string - your hand is not restricted to a particular place.

The next exercise illustrates the fingering to use when only a three-fret range is necessary. Notice how the fourth finger is used, rather than the third, since it involves less tension and gives more control:

STRING	G			D			A			E			A			D			
FINGER	1	2	4	1	2	4	1	2	4	1	2	4	1	2	4	1	2	4	:

Check that all the notes are evenly spaced.

Now play the same exercise but "hammer on". This involves only picking the first note on each string. Bringing down the second and fourth fingers of the left hand firmly behind the frets produces the other two. This works better at speed - so play it as fast as you can

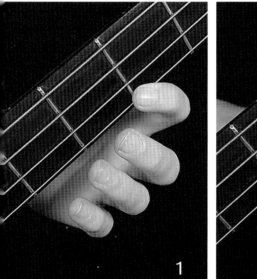

1   2   4

The last exercise in this section is very simple but very important.

Play a rhythm repeating one note - the third fret of the A-string is ideal - keeping the finger pressed down so that the note is sustained. Play this for a while and remember how much finger pressure you're using to hold the string down.

Now start again without pressure on the string - only touch it. Then gradually increase the pressure until there is just enough to produce a clear note. How much pressure are you using now compared with before? Probably much less.

The extra pressure is balanced by extra pressure from your thumb and your hand grips the neck. This reduces your fluency, your hand gets tired and muscles start to ache. If you recognise these symptoms then practise relaxing your technique.

Minimum pressure also means that when you want to 'cut' a note, by releasing the pressure on the string, only a slight alteration is needed - so you have more immediate control.

fingerboard

There are two points to remember in this section:
• Don't just learn the fingerboard - understand it.
• Think across the strings and not just along them.

Most basses have four strings: G, D, A and E. The note produced at the fifth fret of any string is the same as that produced by the next higher open string, so:

• The fifth fret of the E-string (5E) equals open A (0A).
• The fifth fret of the A-string (5A) equals open D (0D).
• The fifth fret of the D-string (5D) equals open G (0G).

This also provides a method of tuning the strings relative to each other - adjust each pair so that they produce the same note. Tuning is covered in the next section using a method that is easier, quicker and more accurate.

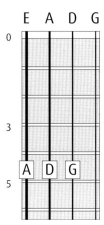

Only seven letters are used in musical notation:

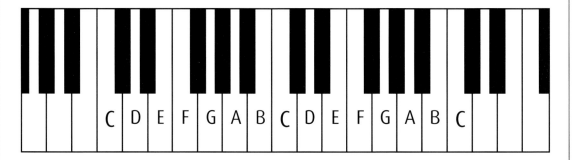

In this example the second set of notes starting from C is an octave (eight notes) higher than the first set - and the sequence extends in both directions. Notes an octave apart, although obviously different in pitch, are closely related and have the same letter name. If possible listen to octaves played on a keyboard.

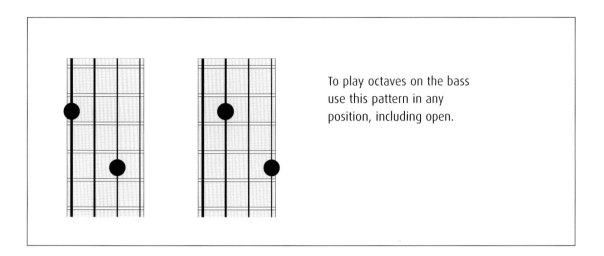

To play octaves on the bass use this pattern in any position, including open.

Octaves are usually played with first and fourth fingers rather than first and third or second and fourth.

Now, whenever you find a note you immediately know another - its octave, either higher or lower. This diagram adds octaves to the notes already included.

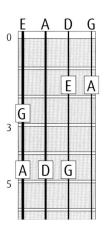

To add the remaining notes it is necessary to understand the 'musical alphabet'. On a keyboard there are no black keys between E/F and B/C and so on the bass these notes are one fret (a semitone) apart. C/D, D/E, F/G and A/B are separated by black keys so they are two frets (a tone) apart. Now the notes B, C and F can be added.

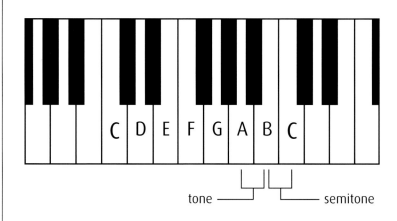

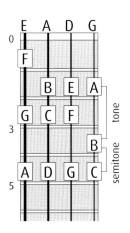

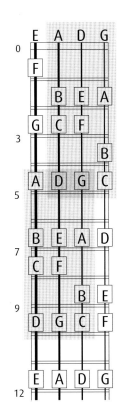

In this diagram the notes in the shaded areas are identical, since ascending from 5E produces the same sequence of notes as ascending from 0A. The same is true for any pair of adjacent strings.

When a note is raised by a semitone it is sharpened (♯):

2G to 3G - A to A♯

When a note is lowered by a semitone it is flattened (♭):

4G to 3G - B to B♭

So the notes corresponding to the black keys have both a sharp and a flat name. There is no need to include these in the diagram, since if you know where a note is, then it is clear where it its sharp and flat are.

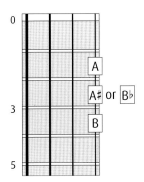

Above the twelfth fret the pattern is repeated an octave higher.

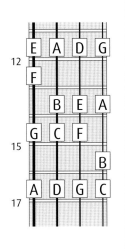

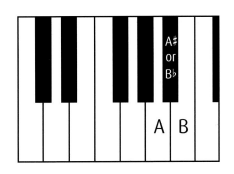

fretted note

harmonic

tuning

If you don't yet have an amplifier leave this section until later and use the fifth-fret method mentioned earlier.

A better method of tuning uses harmonics. These are explained in detail in section **5.3** - for now all you need to know is how to play them. So, while picking an open G-string touch it directly above - not behind - the twelfth fret.

Experiment to discover the exact point to touch the string and the amount of finger pressure required. Too little pressure allows the open string to sound and too much mutes the harmonic. Harmonics are also found over the seventh, fifth and fourth frets on all the strings.

Harmonics will sound clearer if you:

• Pick close to the bridge.
• Select the back (bridge) pickup.
• Use new roundwound strings.

Tuning with harmonics is better because:

• They continue to sound when you take your left hand away to adjust the machine head - so you can hear the effect of your adjustment as you make it.

• They don't depend on frets being accurately positioned or the bridge being correctly adjusted.

• They are higher, purer sounds. This makes tuning easier and more accurate.

A tuning fork produces an ideal reference note because:

• It is accurate. Use a fork marked 'A440' - this is concert pitch, an international standard, and it relates to harmonics found on the bass.

• It can be amplified so that you can hear both fork and harmonic at the same time and from the same place.

With the bass in position, hold the fork in the right hand and strike it on your knee.

While the fork is ringing pick the harmonic at the seventh fret of the D-string (H7D).

Now bring the tuning fork close enough to the pickup so that the sounds are balanced and can be compared. Notice that the A440 tuning fork note is an octave higher than H7D.

If the bass is already almost in tune - if necessary use the fifth-fret method to achieve this - you will hear 'beats'. These are regular pulses in the sound that should slow down and then stop as you adjust the tuning. If the beats get faster you are turning the machine head in the wrong direction. Once tuned the bass should only need slight adjustment and so the beats will be heard clearly.

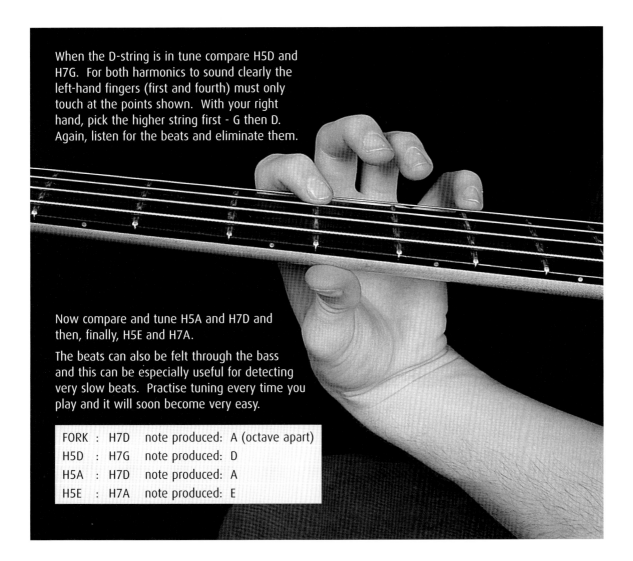

When the D-string is in tune compare H5D and H7G. For both harmonics to sound clearly the left-hand fingers (first and fourth) must only touch at the points shown. With your right hand, pick the higher string first - G then D. Again, listen for the beats and eliminate them.

Now compare and tune H5A and H7D and then, finally, H5E and H7A.

The beats can also be felt through the bass and this can be especially useful for detecting very slow beats. Practise tuning every time you play and it will soon become very easy.

FORK	:	H7D	note produced:	A (octave apart)
H5D	:	H7G	note produced:	D
H5A	:	H7D	note produced:	A
H5E	:	H7A	note produced:	E

Some final points:

• If you are playing with keyboards then tune H5A and H7D to the note A below middle C. If not, then once you are sure of your tuning, tune the other instruments to the bass, since it holds its tuning and is easily tuned accurately.

• If your bass has only one pickup near the neck you may not be able to hear fifth-fret harmonics. In this case use twelfth-fret harmonics instead, and tune in octaves:

> H12D : H7G
> H12A : H7D
> H12E : H7A

• Tuning will be more reliable if you begin with the strings slightly flat and tune them up to the correct pitch.

• An alternative way to hear the tuning fork is to strike it and then place the end between your teeth.

• With a tuner use fifth-fret harmonics. These produce the notes two octaves above the open strings. Use the right hand to mute the strings not being tuned. It is important to learn to tune by ear, so initially only use the tuner to check your accuracy.

notation

Music is notated by placing symbols on a stave.

Both the lines and the spaces are used. A higher position on the stave indicates higher pitch.

The clef determines which notes the lines and spaces represent. The bass clef is used for the bass.

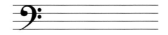

The bass clef corresponds to the letter F and so the line between its dots represents the note F. From this the other notes follow alphabetically.

Don't just memorise this - understand it. If you know the position of one note then the ones above and below are obvious. So knowing where F is makes it clear where G and E are.

Leger lines extend the range of the stave. Usually only one is required below the stave since this corresponds to the lowest note (E) on most basses.

For basses with string/s tuned lower than E, additional notes are required.

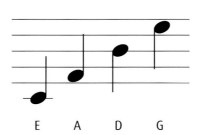

E   A   D   G

The positions of the open strings on the stave have been indicated to enable you to play any note in the correct octave. For instance, F:

1E   **3D(or 8A or 13E)**

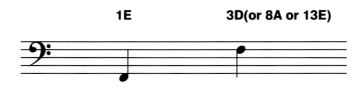

Finally, in keyboard music you may see even lower bass notes. You can play these notes because bass parts are written an octave higher than they sound, so that most notes are on the stave rather than on leger lines below it.

Written   Sounds

If you read a keyboard part and treat it as a bass part then you will sound an octave lower than the keyboard. Any notes that are too low can be played an octave higher and they will then be in the same octave as the keyboard.

electric bass guitar | section two

scales and chords
basics

major scale

To play this scale follow the fingering indicated on the diagram. This involves using the position playing developed earlier. For simplicity the stave shows a C scale - no sharps or flats. Because open strings are not used the pattern can be played in any position. The first note gives the scale its name.

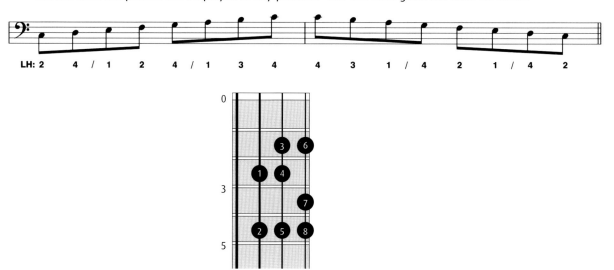

The scale should sound familiar. Once you can play it fluently you can progress to the next exercise which involves going one step beyond the octave to include the ninth - the note an octave above the second.

Starting at 3A, and finishing on 7G, there are five ways to play this - only shifting position once and, again, avoiding open strings. The strokes (/) indicate where you change string. Shift position by two frets when the same finger is used for consecutive notes.

1134/14/124
24/1224/124
24/1244/124
24/124/1124
24/124/1344

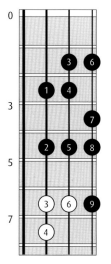

Practise playing up and down continually switching between the options.

Now add two alternatives:

• Two shifts:
1134/1134/1

• Extended fingering - reaching over five frets rather than four:
124/124/124

Starting from 8E the exercise can be played either in position, or using any of the seven patterns already mentioned.

Even more fingerings are possible by starting with the fourth finger.

The following exercise is simply a C scale played in different positions. The shifts are achieved by alternately extending and contracting the hand:

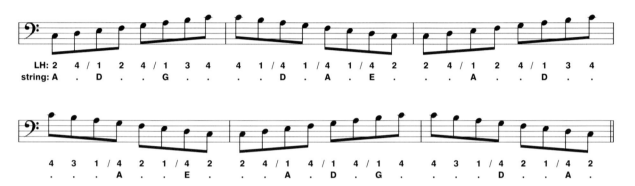

| LH: | 2 | | 4 / 1 | 2 | 4 / 1 | | 3 | 4 | | 4 | 1 / 4 | | 1 / 4 | | 1 / 4 | | 2 | | 2 | | 4 / 1 | 2 | 4 / 1 | | 3 | 4 |
| string: | A | . | D | . | . G | . | . | . | . | . | . D | . | A | . | E | . | . | . | . A | . | . D | . | . |

| 4 | 3 | | 1 / 4 | 2 | 1 / 4 | | 2 | | 2 | | 4 / 1 | | 4 / 1 | | 4 / 1 | | 4 | | 4 | 3 | | 1 / 4 | 2 | 1 / 4 | | 2 |
| . | . | . | . A | . | . E | . | . | . | . A | . | D | . | G | . | . | . | . | . | . D | . | . A | . |

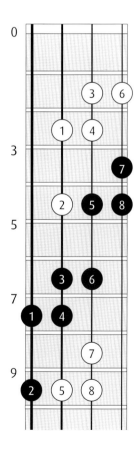

Open strings have been avoided so that:

• The patterns can be used in any position.

• The duration of notes can be controlled with the left hand - releasing the pressure on the string, while maintaining contact to mute it, cuts a note.

thirds

This exercise introduces thirds - pairs of alternate notes from the scale:

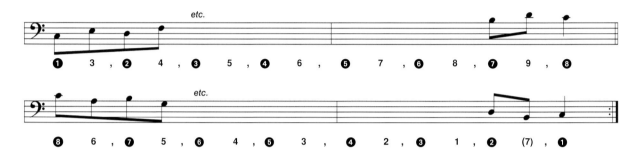

❶   3 , ❷   4 , ❸   5 , ❹   6 , ❺   7 , ❻   8 , ❼   9 , ❽

❽   6 , ❼   5 , ❻   4 , ❺   3 , ❹   2 , ❸   1 , ❷   (7) , ❶

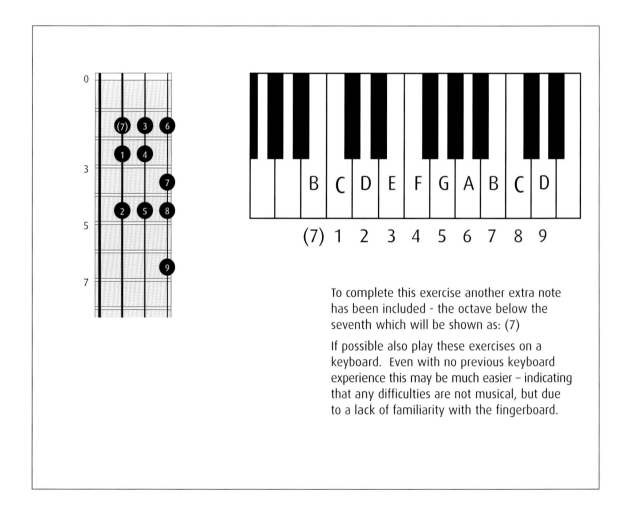

(7) 1 2 3 4 5 6 7 8 9

To complete this exercise another extra note has been included - the octave below the seventh which will be shown as: (7)

If possible also play these exercises on a keyboard. Even with no previous keyboard experience this may be much easier – indicating that any difficulties are not musical, but due to a lack of familiarity with the fingerboard.

Now four-note patterns based on thirds:

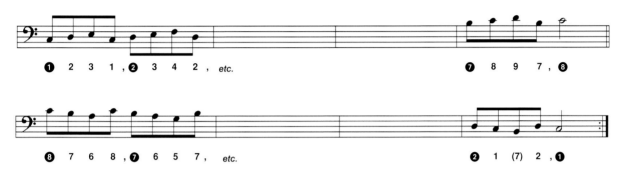

❶ 2 3 1 , ❷ 3 4 2 , *etc.* ❼ 8 9 7 , ❽

❽ 7 6 8 , ❼ 6 5 7 , *etc.* ❷ 1 (7) 2 , ❶

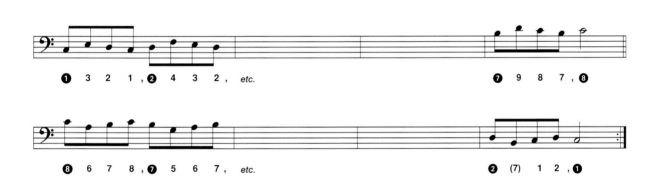

❶ 3 2 1 , ❷ 4 3 2 , *etc.* ❼ 9 8 7 , ❽

❽ 6 7 8 , ❼ 5 6 7 , *etc.* ❷ (7) 1 2 , ❶

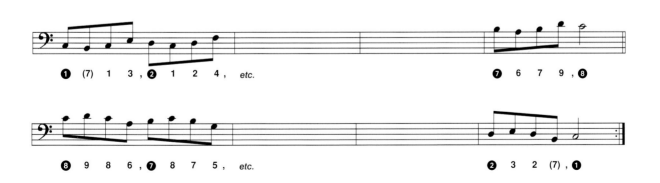

❶ (7) 1 3 , ❷ 1 2 4 , *etc.* ❼ 6 7 9 , ❽

❽ 9 8 6 , ❼ 8 7 5 , *etc.* ❷ 3 2 (7) , ❶

For a variation on the first sequence play alternate pairs reversed:

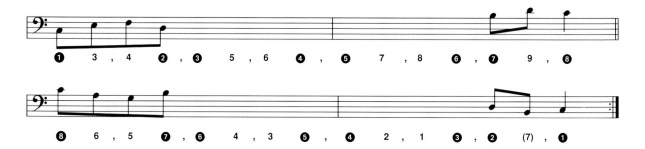

❶   3 , 4   ❷ , ❸   5 , 6   ❹ , ❺   7 , 8   ❻ , ❼   9 , ❽

❽   6 , 5   ❼ , ❻   4 , 3   ❺ , ❹   2 , 1   ❸ , ❷   (7) , ❶

Thirds played an octave higher are called tenths and can be found in section **5.2**.

Now play sixths. In C start at 8E:

❶   6   1 , ❷   7   2 ,   *etc.*

To descend, either start at 5G or an octave higher at 17G:

❽   3   8 , ❼   2   7 ,   *etc.*

If you haven't played exercises like this before, you'll need to spend some time on them to achieve reasonable speed and fluency. They involve all the areas that need developing:

- Technique
- Understanding
- Listening

Use your ears to check your accuracy, but to know if you're correct you must have an exact idea of what you're expecting to hear. This is one reason for using 'etc.' - you should know what comes next without having it spelt out. It also avoids a lot of unnecessary and confusing notation. Using numbers rather than letters is also important. It means that you can think and play these exercises in any scale.

The major scale can be played over two octaves using the indicated fingering. Shift position where consecutive notes are played with the same finger:

1134/1134/134/1134

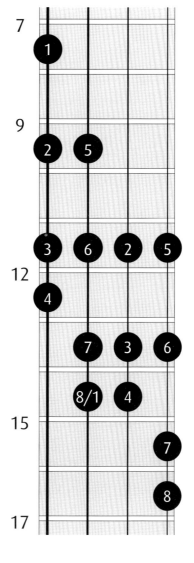

Thirds can be played over two octaves following the same note positions. Use extended fingering where necessary:

Now it's time to consider the structure of the scale in more detail. Play it on the bass - or if possible on a keyboard where it's easier to visualise - and notice that the steps are not equal:

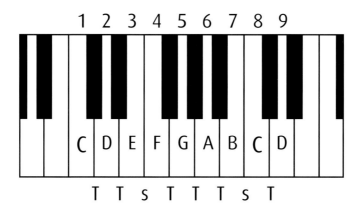

Most of the steps are tones (T) - with the exceptions of 3-4 (E-F) and 7-8 (B-C) which are semitones (s).

Now calculate how 'big' the thirds are by adding together the scale steps. Because the scale is made up of unequal steps - either smaller (semitone) or larger (tone) - it follows that there are two types of third. The larger (4 semitones) is a major third, and the smaller (3 semitones) is a minor third.

THIRDS	SCALE STEPS		SEMITONES	TYPE
1 3	T	T	4	MAJOR
2 4	T	s	3	minor
3 5	s	T	3	minor
4 6	T	T	4	MAJOR
5 7	T	T	4	MAJOR
6 8	T	s	3	minor
7 9	s	T	3	minor

An interval is the 'distance' between a pair of notes. So far four intervals have been introduced:

• Octaves - equivalent to "eighths". They are always the same size - twelve semitones.

• Seconds (between adjacent notes in the scale), thirds and sixths - all occur as major and minor.

Sevenths - which will be introduced later - also occur as major and minor. Fourths and fifths also appear in two varieties, but different words are used to describe them.

triads

A chord is a combination of notes, and a triad is a chord of three notes spaced in thirds - alternate notes from the scale - so in the scale of C: C E G, D F A, E G B, etc. The note the chord is built on is its root and the other notes are its third and fifth respectively.

Much of the music you hear and play is built on chord sequences derived from the scale. Essentially the base line is built around the notes of each chord. So it's important to understand both the structures of the different chord types and also their relation to the scale.

The thirds in the previous section were incomplete triads. To complete each triad a fifth must be added. Still use the scale as the source of notes and keep thirds in mind. Again this is easier to visualise on a keyboard. Move the root/third/fifth pattern along the scale of C, forming a chord on each note in turn. Now play the same chords on the bass:

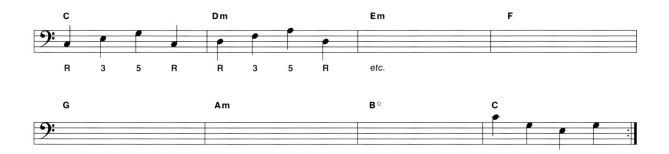

Starting from 3A involves shifting position, since the highest note required is at 10G. So begin at 8E and then the whole sequence can be played in one position.

Most chords are named according to their type of third - major chords have major thirds and minor chords have minor thirds.

Roman numerals are used to indicate which scale note is the root of the chord: I, IV and V are major chords; II, III and VI are minor chords.

It is important to realise that the VII chord contains a different type of fifth. All the other chords have 'perfect' fifths. The fifth in the VII chord is a semitone lower - diminished - and this gives the chord its name.

CHORD TYPE	STRUCTURE	POSITION	CHORDS IN C
MAJOR	R 3 5	I IV V	C F G
MINOR	R m3 5	II III VI	Dm Em Am
DIMINISHED	R m3 °5	VII	B°

m = minor   ° = diminished

In order to play these chords in a low position, and without much shifting, play the fifths an octave lower. Then the fifths, unless diminished, are found on the same fret as the root but one string lower.

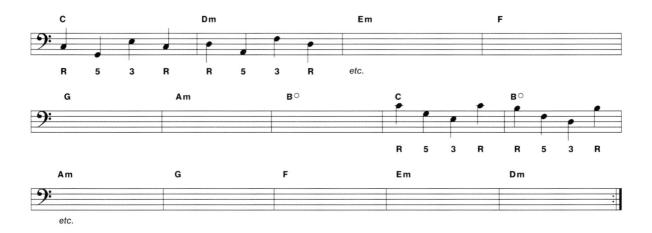

For the ascending part use this fingering:

2212 4314 1141 2212 4324 1141 3141 2

This requires more movement than basic position playing but is more relaxed. In the descending section the thirds are played below the root, and correspond to the sixths introduced in the previous section.

Practising the various chord patterns in different ways should encourage you to introduce more variety into your own playing. It's essential that you get some playing experience - so find some other musicians to learn with.

seventh chords

These are four-note chords produced by adding an extra note to the triads and still using steps of a third: root, third, fifth and seventh. So in the scale of C: CEGB, DFAC, EGBD, etc.

Initially it will be easier to play the sevenths down an octave to avoid high positions. Since a seventh is the scale note below the octave it follows that, played lower, it's the scale note below the root - so, again in C: the seventh of C is B, the seventh of D is C, etc.

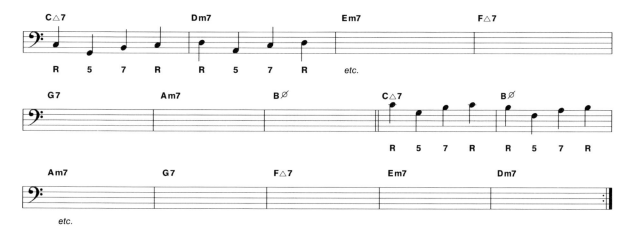

The thirds have been omitted in order to focus attention on the sevenths.

Only two chords in the scale have major sevenths - because there are only two semitone steps in the scale. Adding Δ7 to the basic chord symbol indicates a major seventh. All the other chords have minor sevenths, and adding 7 to the chord symbol represents this. For the diminished chord this is written ∅.

As with the intervals introduced previously, there are two types of seventh:

• MAJOR: higher - a semitone below the octave/root.
• MINOR: lower - a tone below the octave/root.

So there are four types of seventh chords in the scale:

CHORD TYPE	STRUCTURE				POSITION			CHORDS IN C
MAJOR SEVENTH	R	3	5	Δ7	I	IV		CΔ7 FΔ7
(DOMINANT) SEVENTH	R	3	5	m7	V			G7
MINOR SEVENTH	R	m3	5	m7	II	III	VI	Dm7 Em7 Am7
HALF-DIMINISHED	R	m3	°5	m7	VII			BØ

The V chord is referred to as a dominant seventh because it only occurs on the fifth or dominant note of the scale.

The VII chord is called 'half-diminished' to distinguish it from another chord - the diminished seventh - which does not occur in the major scale and will be introduced later.

Now play seventh chords up and down the scale using a variety of patterns:

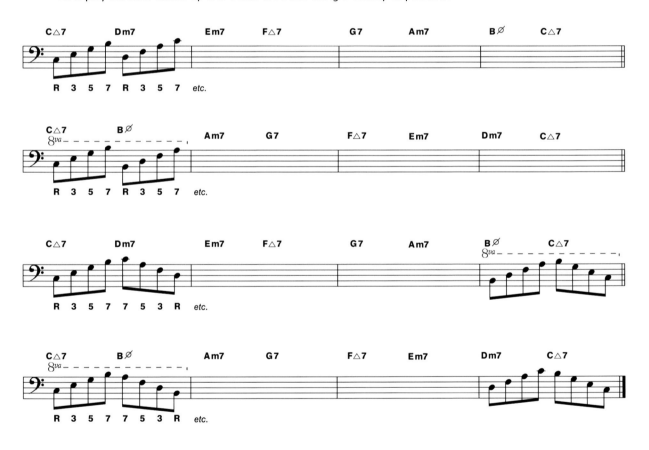

'8va' means play an octave higher than written.

There are many ways of playing these exercises. Begin by playing all the roots on the A-string - use the second finger when there's a major third and the first when there's a minor third. This involves playing over the whole fingerboard and will help to familiarise you with high positions.

An alternative approach, which is useful for comparing the shapes of the different chords, is to play them all on the same root:

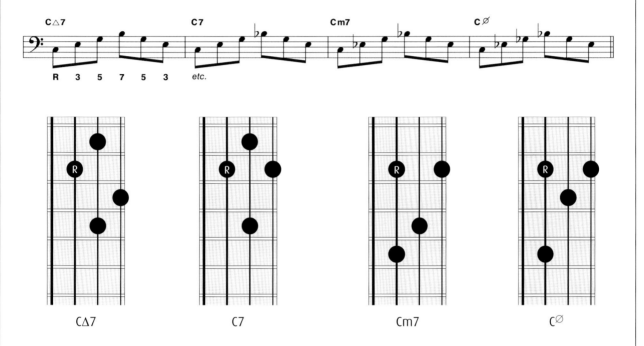

CΔ7   C7   Cm7   CØ

This makes less musical sense because each chord is from a different scale -
CΔ7 is in C (I) or G (IV)
C7 is in F (V)
Cm7 is in B♭ (II), A♭ (III) or E♭ (VI)
CØ is in D♭ (VII)

Finally the chords can be extended to include ninths - which are a third above sevenths. So in C: CEGBD, DFACE, EGBDF, etc.

Ninths are usually a tone above the octave - major ninths. In two cases (III and VII) they are a semitone lower - minor ninths - which is indicated in a chord symbol as ♭9. However in practice the ♭9 is not added to these chords since it would confuse their function (see section **3.2**).

So far each chord note has occurred in two forms. Therefore the more notes included the more types of chord there are: three triads, four sevenths, five ninths, six elevenths and seven thirteenths - and that's the limit because then all seven notes of the scale have been used.

chord symbols

Chord symbols provide a simple way for musicians to communicate without having to use notation. The V chord is treated as standard so, unless specified, thirds are major and sevenths are minor. Any extensions or alterations must be indicated.

	R	3	5	7	9	11	13
G7	G	B	D	F			
G9	G	B	D	F	A		
G11	G	B	D	F	A	C	
G13	G	B	D	F	A	C	E

Minor chords are usually indicated by 'm', although 'mi', 'min' and '-' are also used.

	R	3	5	7	9	11	13
Gm7	G	Bb	D	F			
Gm9	G	Bb	D	F	A		
Gm11	G	Bb	D	F	A	C	
Gm13	G	Bb	D	F	A	C	E

If the chord includes a major seventh then 'Δ' or 'maj' must be added:

	R	3	5	7	9	11	13
GΔ7	G	B	D	F#			
GΔ9	G	B	D	F#	A		
GΔ11	G	B	D	F#	A	C	
GΔ13	G	B	D	F#	A	C	E

Chords can include sixths:

	R	3	5	6	9
G6	G	B	D	E	
G6/9	G	B	D	E	A

In suspended chords an adjacent scale note replaces the third:

G7sus4	G	C	D	F
G7sus2	G	A	D	F

Other variations are indicated as alterations, for example:

	R	3	5	7	9	11	13
G7♭5	G	B	D♭	F			
G7♭9	G	B	D	F	A♭		
G13♯11	G	B	D	F	A	C♯	E

The half-diminished chord (∅) is also written as m7♭5. It corresponds to the top notes of a G9 chord:

	R	3	5	7
B∅	B	D	F	A

The augmented seventh (+7) and diminished seventh (°7) chords will be introduced in section **3.3**.

electric bass guitar | section three

scales and chords
advanced

modes

Play the notes of the C scale, but start and finish on D. This sequence of notes is a mode of the original scale and in this case relates to a Dm7 chord - the II chord in the key of C. However, when Dm7 occurs in other keys - Bb (III) or F (VI) - it will require the notes of the corresponding scale and consequently the modes will be slightly different.

Alternatively think of the mode as the chord with all its extensions - ninth, eleventh and thirteenth. Although Dm7 is obviously the same whatever key it's in, the extensions will vary. To add extra scale notes beyond the fixed root/third/fifth/seventh it's necessary to take account of the key. Modes are a useful way of organising that information.

Any confusion associated with modes is largely the result of names that are complicated and often unnecessary. This is resolved by applying the same Roman numerals used to identify the chords. So Dm7 is the II chord in C and it corresponds to the II mode - this also has the advantage of making the connection between chord and mode completely obvious.

The following chart shows the seven modes of a C scale and relates each mode to its chord:

- Start each mode on the A-string with the second finger where there's a major third (I, IV, V) and the first where the third is minor (II, III, VI and VII).
- The II mode can't be played in position - use this fingering: 134/14/124.

Every mode is different and each corresponds to a seven-note chord - there are seven of these - and so playing modes is a good exercise because repeated patterns can't be used. Playing the whole sequence involves a two-octave range and so helps to develop both technique and fingerboard knowledge.

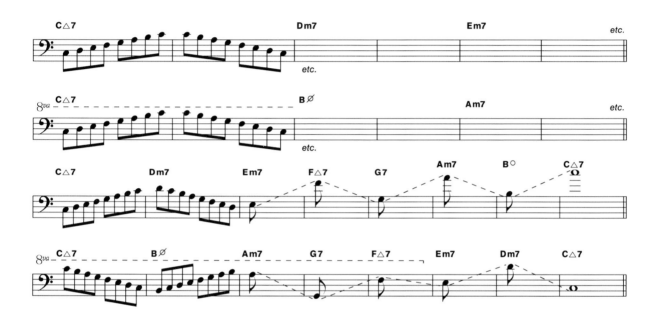

It's also useful to play different modes starting from the same root. Modes I, IV and V starting from C relate to C chords in the keys of C, G and F. The V mode includes a minor seventh - as does the V chord - and the IV mode features an augmented fourth (+4) - a semitone higher than the usual perfect fourth. The following diagrams illustrate these points:

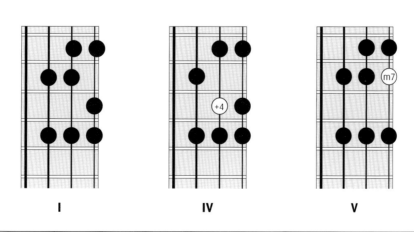

All this information can be shown on one diagram. The solid notes are in the same positions in all three modes whereas the open notes vary.

This shows that there is a five-note pattern that will fit any of the major chords in the scale. The other notes - fourths and sevenths - require more caution because:

• Their positions vary.
• They may clash with chord notes - apart from the minor seventh, they're only a semitone from chord notes.

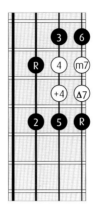

Now repeat the same process for the minor modes. The VI mode has been placed first because it corresponds to a minor scale. In comparison, the II mode contains a major sixth and the III mode a minor second.

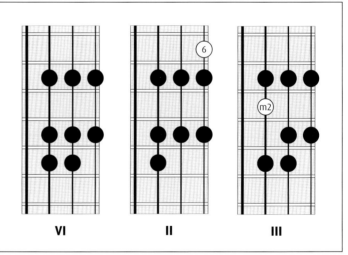

VI   II   III

This can be illustrated on one diagram. Again there's a five-note pattern and it fits any of the minor chords in the scale. However, it's now seconds and sixths that may cause problems - varying positions and semitone clashes.

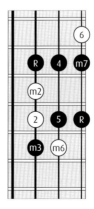

These patterns are often referred to as 'pentatonic (five-note) scales'. However, moving a pattern to each primary chord in turn involves all seven notes of the major scale and, therefore, is not pentatonic:

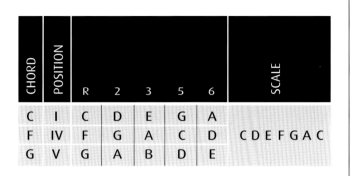

CHORD	POSITION	R	2	3	5	6	SCALE
C	I	C	D	E	G	A	
F	IV	F	G	A	C	D	C D E F G A C
G	V	G	A	B	D	E	

This chart includes all the intervals found in a major scale:

INTERVAL	m2	2	m3	3	4	+4	°5	5	m6	6	m7	7	octave
SEMITONES	1	2	3	4	5	6		7	8	9	10	11	12

• Seconds, thirds, sixths and sevenths are major unless shown as minor (m).
• Minor intervals are always a semitone smaller than major intervals.
• Fourths and fifths are perfect unless augmented (+) or diminished (°).

The confusion often associated with modes has been avoided by applying Roman numerals when modes relate to the chords in a key. The names, however, are appropriate when the modes are used as scales in their own right.

Even though the II mode and the Dorian mode contain the same sequence of notes they have different meanings. The II mode is associated with the II chord which will eventually resolve to the I chord. The Dorian mode is associated with the same chord but without that implication.

I	Ionian
II	Dorian
III	Phrygian
IV	Lydian
V	Mixolydian
VI	Aeolian
VII	Locrian

Originally modes formed the basis of medieval church music. Later, however, the major (Ionian) and minor (Aeolian, but slightly altered) became the most widely used, because only they provided the V/I (dominant/tonic) resolution which is now the basis of tonal music.

In tonal music a scale is the basic source of notes for both melody and harmony. Consequently the note-pattern is different for each chord. Modern use of modes often involves a fixed note-pattern being shifted from chord to chord. For example, a blues sequence is tonal - I, IV, V in a major key - but each chord is a dominant seventh corresponding to the Mixolydian mode. In the melody, however, the third is often flattened resulting in a Dorian mode. These two modes occur the most. The Dorian is often the basis for improvisation as there are no awkward notes a semitone above the chord notes.

chord function

In the following sections seventh chords are indicated. In practice a chord may occur as a simple triad, or in a more complex form with its extensions.

The scale chords have been given numbers - I, II, III, etc. - but they also have names. Generally only three of these are used:

TONIC (I)   SUBDOMINANT (IV)   DOMINANT (V)

These are the most basic chords in the scale. They are called primary chords. Together they produce a sense of key - they contain all of the notes of the scale. Music in the key of C will usually feature the primary chords - CΔ7, FΔ7 and G7. Listen to these chords and notice how the dominant chord leads back to the tonic. To understand why a dominant chord has this effect it's necessary to consider the structure of the different types of chord:

MAJOR SEVENTH	I, IV	R	5	3	Δ7
DOMINANT SEVENTH	V	R	5	3	m7
MINOR SEVENTH	II, III, VI	R	5	m3	m7
HALF-DIMINISHED	VII	R	°5	m3	m7

The chord notes have been arranged to show that each contains two intervals of a fifth. Only the V and VII chords, however, include a diminished fifth interval - from major third to minor seventh and from root to diminished fifth - and so both of these chords have a dominant function.

When a dominant chord resolves to the tonic the tension of the diminished fifth interval is released with both notes moving by semitone steps.

Now a simple sequence which alternates between tonic (I) and dominant (V).

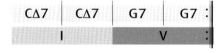

The subdominant chord (IV) may be included to lead to the dominant.

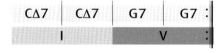

Chords a third apart in the scale are very similar. They share three notes and, provided they have the same function, they may be substituted for one another. In the case of the IV chord the alternative is the II chord.

The advantage of this version is that there is now a sequence of fourths in the roots - D > G > C. This produces a stronger progression.

Finally there are the tonic function chords - obviously I, but also the similar III and VI. These alternatives can be included to vary and extend the sequence.

Notice how the notes in one chord lead to those in the next. Where the progression moves in fourths - E > A > D > G > C - the third and fifth of each chord lead to the root of the next.

TONIC	TONIC	SUBDOMINANT	DOMINANT
CΔ7	Am7	Dm7	G7
I	VI	II	V
Em7	Am7	Dm7	G7
III	VI	II	V

This chart contains all the information on chord function:

	POSITION	CHORDS IN C	CHORD NOTES	REQUIRED NOTES
TONIC	I	CΔ7	C E G B	
	III	Em7	E G B D	No F
	VI	Am7	A C E G	
SUBDOMINANT	IV	FΔ7	**F** A **C** E	F & C (not B)
	II	Dm7	D **F** A **C**	
DOMINANT	V	G7	G **B** D **F**	F & B (not C)
	VII	Bø	**B** D **F** A	

All this is of special significance to the bass player as it shows that:

• A fourth confuses the function of major and dominant chords.

• The most important distinction between chords of the same function is the bass note. So CΔ7 with A in the bass produces Am9. This is a simple way of producing more complex chords. It also creates a more subtle and interesting sound as it avoids duplication of the bass note. When the bass note is another chord note - the third, fifth or seventh - then the result is called inversion. In this case it would be written:

CΔ7/E   CΔ7/G   CΔ7/B

Similar notation is used to indicate other chords. For example, the top four notes of G11 form Dm7.
So combining a Dm7 chord with a G bass note produces G11. This would be written: Dm7/G.
This chord is not an inversion because:

• Dm7 does not contain the note G.
• G is the root of the G11 chord.

It is similar to a suspended chord - no third - and has a similar function which, although its root is the
dominant, is subdominant. This is because:

• It does not include a diminished fifth interval.
• It leads to the dominant (V) and a resolution to the tonic (I):

Dm7/G	G7	CΔ7
II/V	V	I

Sometimes chords are 'misspelt' and need a different bass note to clarify their function - minor sixth
chords are an example. When one occurs as the II chord of a major key it is a dominant chord in
disguise. This is because it contains a diminished fifth interval between the minor third and the major
sixth. The change of bass note removes any confusion:

Dm7	Dm6/G	CΔ7
Dm7	G9	CΔ7
II	V	I

An alternative here would be:

Dm7/G	Dm6/G	CΔ7
G11	G9	CΔ7
II/V	V	I

Minor sixth chords will not usually occur on Em (III) or Am (VI) since their sixths - the notes C# and F# -
are not in the C scale. Other examples of minor sixth chords involve the minor key and are included in
the next section.

minor key

The VI mode of the major scale corresponds to the natural minor scale. Because this scale contains the same notes, and therefore the same chords, as the major scale it's referred to as the relative minor. So A minor is the relative minor of C major. The reason the VI mode is appropriate - and not II or III - is because the three minor chords then form the familiar I(Am)/IV(Dm)/V(Em) pattern which is the basis of a key.

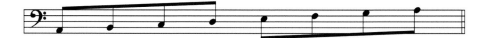

However, in practice a dominant seventh chord is required on V to create the tension that is resolved by returning to the tonic. So the typical chords in A minor would be:

I	II	III	IV	V	VI	VII
Am/Am7	B⌀	CΔ7	Dm7	E7/E+7	FΔ7	G7/G♯°7

The essential difference between the chords in C major and those in A minor is the replacement of Em7 by E7. This involves raising its third from G to G♯ - this change also produces the G♯°7 chord. However, G♮, and not G♯, is required for the other chords.

If the E7 chord in A minor is extended then it may include:

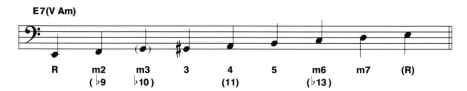

E7(V Am)

R	m2 (♭9)	m3 (♭10)	3	4 (11)	5	m6 (♭13)	m7	(R)

As before, the 11th is usually omitted - see **chord function 3.2**.

This chord contains the minor 9th (F) and minor 13th (C). However, in chord symbols only the third can be described as minor, so it is written: E7♭9♭13. Notice that the 9th and 13th have **not** been altered - they are notes from the scale of A minor.

E7♭9 contains two diminished fifths – G♯>D and B>F. An "edited" version of this chord produces the diminished seventh chord G♯°7. It contains a minor third, diminished fifth and diminished seventh. It is a dominant function chord - occurring on the ♯VII step of the minor scale - which resolves to Am (I). The similar G7 would resolve to C (III).

			R	3	5	m7	m9
V	E7♭9		E	G♯	B	D	F

			R	m3	°5	°7
♯VII	G♯°7		G♯	B	D	F

			R	3	5	m7
♮VII	G7		G	B	D	F

Another version of the V chord in A minor is E7b13. Omitting the fifth produces the augmented chord E+7:

	R	3	5	m7	m13
E7♭13	E	G♯	B	D	C
E+7	E	G♯	(B)	D	C
	R	3		m7	+5

The augmented (+5) or sharpened fifth ("B♯") corresponds to the m6/b13 (C).
A bass line for E+7 can still include the "normal" fifth (B♮).

Although G♯ is required for the E7 chord, G♮ may occur in the melody and/or as an extension. It is often inaccurately described as a ♯9. It is always a ♭10 - a minor third over a dominant chord. As the dominant chord in the minor key this chord may also include the ♭9 and/or the ♭13. However, when it occurs in a blues it is with the ♮9 and ♮13.

Previous chords have contained both major and minor third intervals. However, all the notes of the diminished seventh are a minor third apart. This symmetrical structure means that there are three sets of four chords with the same notes:

G♯°7 = B°7 = D°7 = F°7
A°7 = C°7 = D♯°7 = F♯°7
A♯°7 = C♯°7 = E°7 = G°7

Each one of a set, however, relates to a different dominant seventh chord and is the ♯VII chord of a different minor scale:

G♯°7(♯VII Am)

R   m3   °5   °7   (R)

The notes of an augmented triad - root/third/augmented fifth - are all a major third apart. So there are four groups of three chords with the same notes:

E+	=	G♯+	=	C+
F+	=	A+	=	C♯+
F♯+	=	A♯+	=	D+
G+	=	B+	=	D♯+

The chords in each set contain the same notes. However, each chord relates to a different dominant seventh chord and is the V chord of a different minor key. This is clear when the sevenths are included:

	R	3	+5	m7	KEY
E+7	E	G♯	C	D	Am
G♯+7	G♯	B♯	E	F♯	C♯m
C+7	C	E	A♭	B♭	Fm

Note names - G♯/A♭, B♯/C - vary depending on the key.

The diminished seventh and half-diminished chords share the same diminished triad. The difference is the sevenths - diminished and minor respectively:

		R	m3	°5	°7	m7
♯VII(Am)	G♯°7	G♯	B	D	F	
VII(A)	G♯ø	G♯	B	D		F♯

Notice that when a minor interval is reduced by a semitone it becomes diminished so G♯>F - °7.

If a major interval is increased by a semitone it becomes augmented so F>G♯ - +2.

When a minor sixth chord occurs as the IV chord in a minor key and leads to the V chord it is usually better to interpret it as the II chord:

Dm6	E7	Am
B⌀	E7	Am
II	V	I

In C major the minor sixth chord on IV (Fm6) is from the parallel or tonic minor - in this case from C minor. Fm6 corresponds to D⌀ and they are subdominant minor chords - II or IV from C minor - and can:

• Lead to G7 (the V chord in both keys).
• Return either directly to C△ or to another tonic chord (Em).
• Be played over a G pedal.

Fm6	G7	C△7
D⌀	G7	C△7
D⌀/G	G7	C△7

The subdominant minor chord also occurs as a minor major seventh - Fm$^{\triangle 7}$. Over a B♭ bass note this creates B♭7+11. Either chord tends to lead back, directly or indirectly, to the tonic (I or III):

C△7	F△7	Fm$^{\triangle 7}$	B♭7^{+11}	
Em7	Am7	Dm7	G7	C△7

Each parallel minor chord is associated with a mode of the same scale:

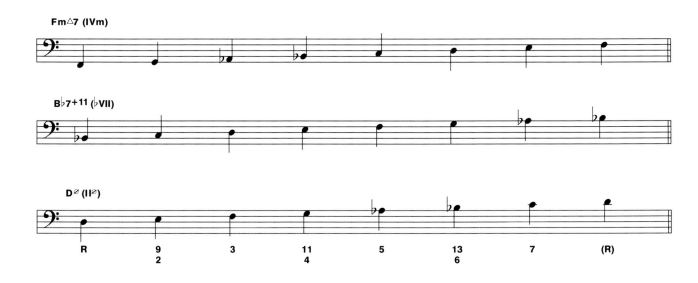

Fm△7 (IVm)

B♭7+11 (♭VII)

D⌀ (II♭)

| R | 9
2 | 3 | 11
4 | 5 | 13
6 | 7 | (R) |

secondary dominants

Normally a dominant chord is a V chord. If this chord occurs elsewhere in the scale it's called a SECONDARY DOMINANT. It will tend to resolve to the chord a fourth above - as if going to a tonic - so, in the key of C:

SCALE CHORD	SECONDARY DOMINANT	RESOLVES TO
Dm7	D7	G7
Am7	A7	Dm7
Em7	E7	Am7
CΔ7	C7	FΔ7

A secondary dominant is produced by altering one note:
• Sharpening the third of a minor seventh chord.
• Flattening the seventh of a major seventh chord.

The following sequence is a variation on an earlier one. This time A7 replaces Am7 to create more tension and a stronger resolution to Dm7:

CΔ7	A7	Dm7	G7	
Em7	A7	Dm7	G7	CΔ7

Here are two variations on this sequence:

CΔ7	E⌀ A7	Dm7	G7	CΔ7

The E⌀ chord functions as "secondary subdominant" creating a "II V" leading to the Dm7.

CΔ7	C#°7	Dm7	G7	CΔ7

Now the A7 chord has been replaced by C#° - implying A7$^{\flat9}$ - to produce a chromatic bass line.

The "secondary II V" progression can also occur:
• Between I and IV:

| CΔ7 | Gm7 C7 | FΔ7 | etc |

• Approaching VI:

| CΔ7 | Bᵒ E7 | Am | E7 | Am7 | D7 | Dm7 | G7 | CΔ7 |

The four bars starting with Am can also occur as:

| | Am | AmΔ7 | Am7 | Am6 | | | |

The bass line may follow the descending chromatic notes: A G♯ G F♯.

Altering all the minor sevenths (III, VI, II) produces this sequence of dominant chords:

| E7 | A7 | D7 | G7 | CΔ7 |

Then each dominant chord may be preceded with its "II" chord:

| Bm7 | E7 | Em7 | A7 | Am7 | D7 | Dm7 | G7 | CΔ7 |
| II | V | II | V | II | V | II | V | I |

Scale   A   D   G   C

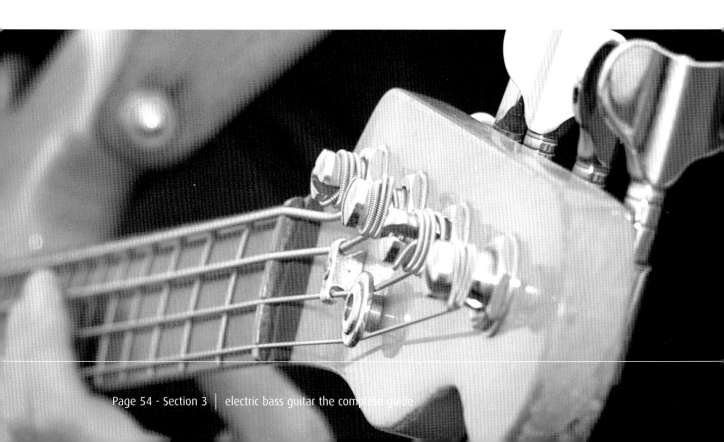

chord substitution

A tritone is an interval of three tones - half an octave. It occurs as a diminished fifth (B ~ F) or an augmented fourth (F ~ B). Tritone substitution of dominant seventh chords is possible because both chords contain the same tritone:

chord	3	7
G7	B	F
C♯7/D♭7	E♯/F	B/C♭

When the dominant seventh chord a tritone away is substituted a progression of fourths becomes chromatic:

| Em7 | A7 | Dm7 | G7 | CΔ7 |

| Em7 | E♭7 | Dm7 | D♭7 | CΔ7 |

A more complete understanding of tritone substitution involves chord function. For dominant function the V chord (G7) avoids the 4th/11th (C), because it implies subdominant function. However, the +11th (C♯) may be added because, since it is not in the scale, it has no functional implications. It also increases tension by introducing another tritone (G ~ C♯). When this alteration is included the V mode becomes:

G7⁺¹¹

Tritone substitution then simply involves 'inverting' the chord with the +11 (C♯) becoming the root. The scale of the extended chord still consists of the same notes:

C♯7alt

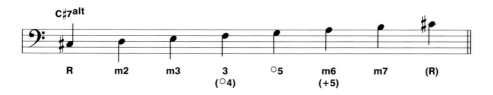

The substitute chord is then C♯7♭5 which is usually labelled D♭7♭5 and often referred to as C♯7alt or D♭7alt - because, compared with a major scale/I chord, every note has been altered (lowered) in relation to the tonic/root. However, it is simpler - and more musically accurate - to realise that only the tonic/root has been altered (raised).

For resolution to a minor chord the positions of the dominant chords are reversed:
In A minor the altered V chord is E7alt:

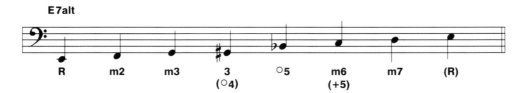

E7alt

R   m2   m3   3   o5   m6   m7   (R)
                             (o4)   (+5)

The tritone substitution is B♭7+11:

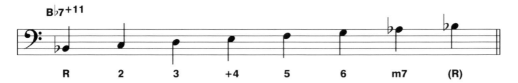

B♭7+11

R   2   3   +4   5   6   m7   (R)

The note names depend on the chord - G♯ corresponds to A♭.

All the scales and modes mentioned so far place chords in a key and make their function clear.
Alternative symmetrical scales are related to the symmetrical diminished and augmented chords.

The Diminished scale occurs in two modes:
- for a dominant seventh chord - a semitone/tone sequence.
- for a diminished seventh chord - a tone/semitone sequence.

E7♭9   R   3   5   7   (R)   ♭9

G♯o7   R   m3   o5   o7   (R)

Both versions are ambiguous because:
- They include the notes (G♯, B, D, F) of the diminished seventh chord/s and the root notes
  (E, G, B♭, C♯) of the four possible dominant seventh chords.
- They avoid the root notes (A, C, E♭, F♯) of the four corresponding tonic minor chords.

- The Whole-Tone scale is a series of tone steps:

E +7

R   3   +5   7   (R)

This scale is tonally ambiguous because:
- It includes the roots (E, G♯, C) and sevenths (D, F♯, B♭) of three augmented chords.
- It avoids the root notes (A, C♯, F) of the corresponding tonic minor chords.

This chart shows the similarities between these different scales:

Dominant (+11)

E7+11

Altered

E7alt

Whole Tone

E +7

Diminished (S/T)

E7♭9

R   3   +4/°5   m7   (R)

The Dominant(+11) and Altered are modes of each other and consist of halves which are diminished and whole-tone.

Finally the Chromatic scale which includes all twelve notes:

LH: 1 2 3 4 / 1 2 3 4 / 1 2 3 4 4 3 2 1 / 4 3 2 1 / 4 3 2 1

electric bass guitar | section four

music
reading

notation

The following symbols are used to indicate the relative duration of notes and rests:

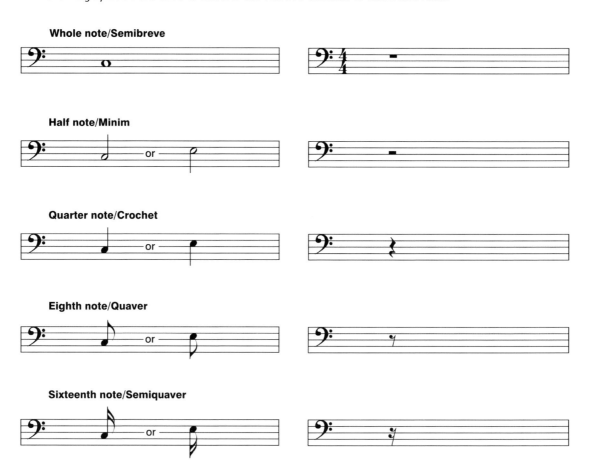

Whole note/Semibreve

Half note/Minim

Quarter note/Crochet

Eighth note/Quaver

Sixteenth note/Semiquaver

Stems can point up or down, but it is usually convenient for notes low on the stave to have their stems upwards, and notes higher on the stave to have their stems downwards.

The time signature is a pair of numbers at the beginning of a piece of music:

The upper number indicates the number of beats or pulses in each bar or measure of music. Tap your foot to music in 4/4 and feel the regular grouping of four beats:

ONE two three four, ONE two three four, etc.

Music in 3/4 will be felt in groups of three beats:

ONE two three, ONE two three, etc.

The lower number of a time signature indicates which note represents the beat. The number '4' represents a quarter-note beat and '2' a half-note beat:

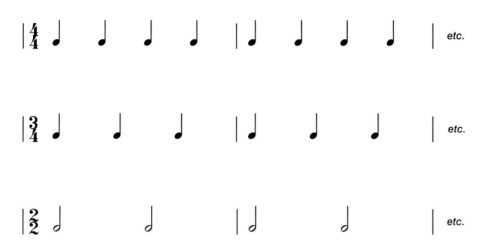

The bar line indicates that the next beat is the beginning of another bar. There is no pause at the end of the bar and no time between the bar line and the first beat of the bar.

rhythm patterns

In this section no tempos are given - a quarter note has no value in terms of seconds, only a value relative to other note lengths in the same piece. So vary the tempos when practising and, initially, aim for control and awareness, rather than speed.

It is good practice to tap rhythms with the right hand - while keeping the beat with a foot - before playing them on the bass. If you are using a pick move it in the same direction as your foot - down-stroke on the beat and up-stroke off the beat - with the eighth notes even and regular.

The approach that follows is very different from the conventional one. It is more musical, less mechanical and corresponds to how readers actually read. The main differences are:

• Pattern recognition rather than counting.
• Initially only considering rhythm - right hand – and not duration - left hand.
• Starting from shorter notes and progressing to longer ones.

Each of the following patterns lasts for half of a ⁴⁄₄ bar - two beats. Follow each with a half rest - two beats' silence - to make a complete bar, which should then be played several times. By repeating this process regularly you will soon learn to recognise the sound and feel of the different patterns, and be able to distinguish between them.

The tails of the eighth notes are grouped to make reading easier and to indicate where the stronger - first and third - beats fall.

To produce the second pattern remove the second note from the first pattern:

Similarly, the third and fourth patterns involve omitting the third and fourth notes respectively:

When two notes of the same pitch are joined together with a tie ⌢ or ⌣, only the first is picked, and the sound is sustained for the duration of both notes:

A dot after a note or rest extends its duration by a half of its value:

The fifth pattern is produced by adding a tie to the second.
The tie can then be replaced with a dot so that:

is written:

To play this, begin with the second pattern and then omit the middle note. This approach does not involve counting or attempting to play a note one and a half beats long - if the eighth note is in the correct place then, provided the dotted note is sustained, it will be the correct length.

The sixth pattern is simply two notes on consecutive beats - check that you are not still playing the fifth pattern.

The seventh pattern corresponds to the first two notes of the first pattern. Make sure that the first note is on the beat.

The eighth pattern is simply a single half note:

Here are the eight patterns arranged so that they can be compared -

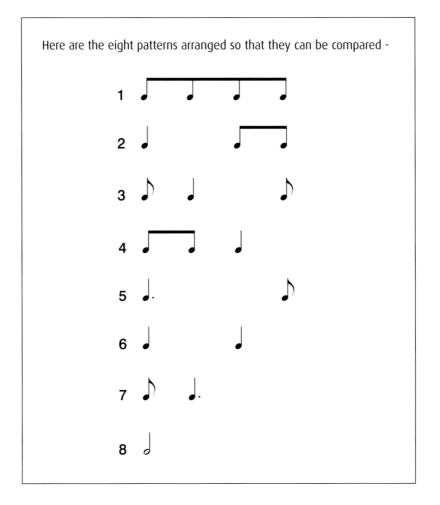

Now play the patterns in sequence, each rest lasts for two beats:

On the CD each track starts with a four-beat "count" followed by eight bars as written.

When you can play all the rhythms accurately check the duration of the notes. Each note should last until, or just before, the following note or rest. So, in the eighth pattern the half note should finish on the third beat. Remember that this is achieved by releasing the pressure of the finger on the string while maintaining contact with it.

On the following pages pairs of patterns are combined to produce complete bars. There are no pauses between the patterns - either in the middle or at the end of a bar. Repeat the bar **1.1** several times to get the idea. Then move on to each bar in turn - again with repeats - and then two, four and eight bar sequences.

Always begin by practising the individual patterns before playing the combinations, and remember that all this can be done without a bass. Just tap the rhythm with your hand while keeping the beat with your foot. Don't separate the two - but be aware of how they relate - and don't count.

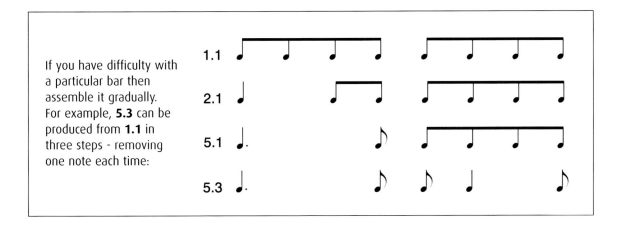

If you have difficulty with a particular bar then assemble it gradually. For example, **5.3** can be produced from **1.1** in three steps - removing one note each time:

When you have completed the first series progress to the sequences with ties. A tie extends a note from one group to the next. A tie from the last note of the first pattern to the first note of the second pattern, involves not playing the first note of the second pattern. A tie over the bar line involves not playing the first note of the following bar.

These rhythms will help you to develop the feel for reading and playing syncopation - the shifting of accents from the beats usually accented. If any bar is a problem then simplify it by removing the tie. Replacing the tie then simply removes one note.

It is important to be able to recognise patterns by ear - so ask someone to play rhythms for you to identify. One of the best ways to improve your reading is to write. So write out all your lines and any ideas you have. This will also help you to remember them, and will encourage you to develop and vary them.

While playing the rhythm patterns that follow you can also add notes from scales or modes. For example for patterns **1.1** to **1.8**:

Then for patterns **2.1 – 2.8** play mode II, **3.1 – 3.8** mode III etc.

Notice the difference in effect when a bar – for example **1.3** - is repeated. Played once, the last note is felt as a syncopated accent. Repeated, it is an unaccented "pick up" which leads to the first beat of the next bar.

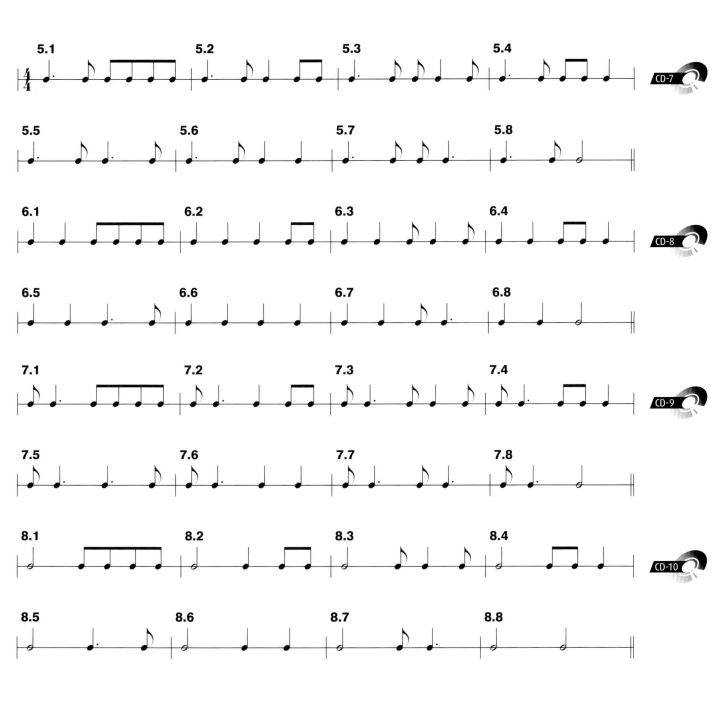

reading music

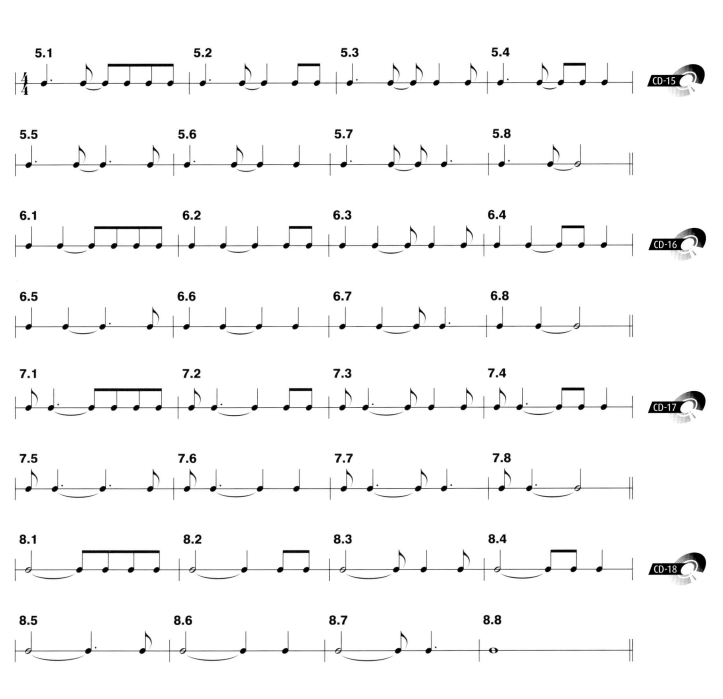

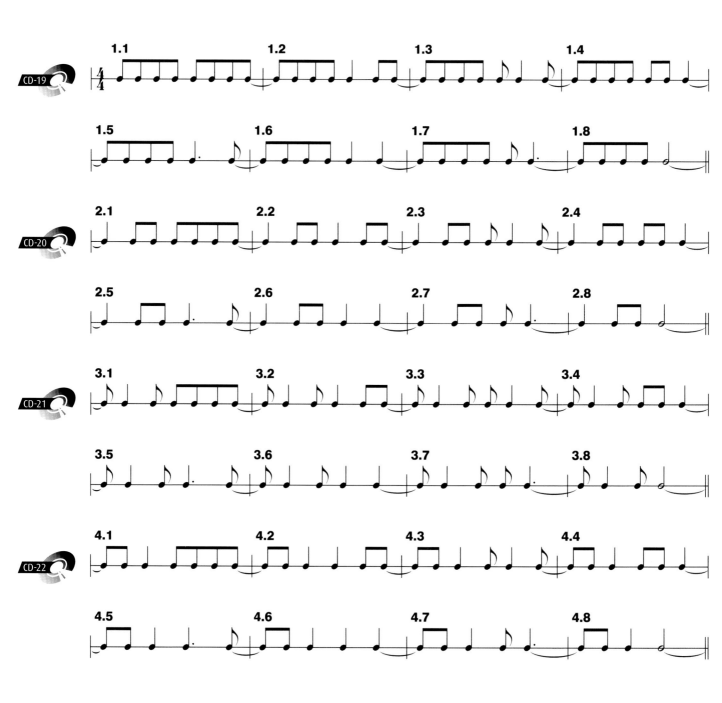

On the CD the the first note of tracks #20-26 is played and not tied as written

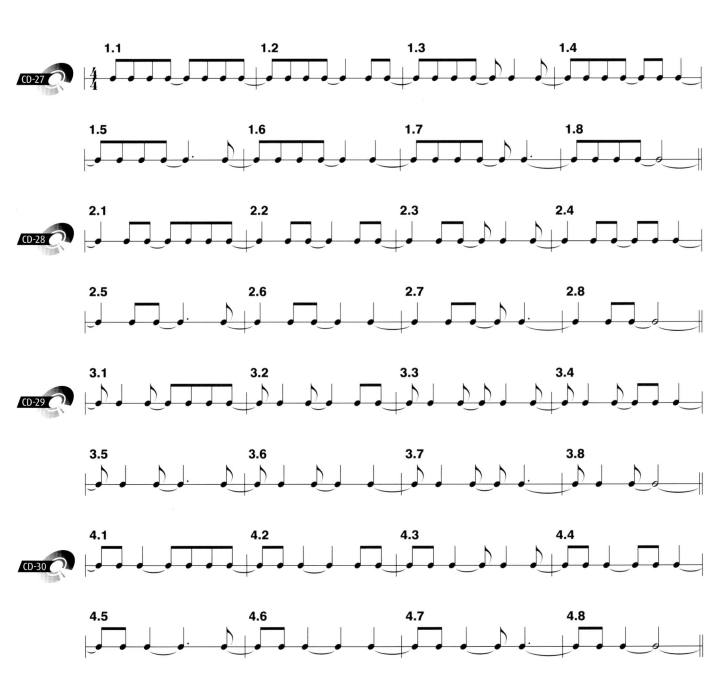

On the CD the first note of tracks #28-34 is played and not tied as written.

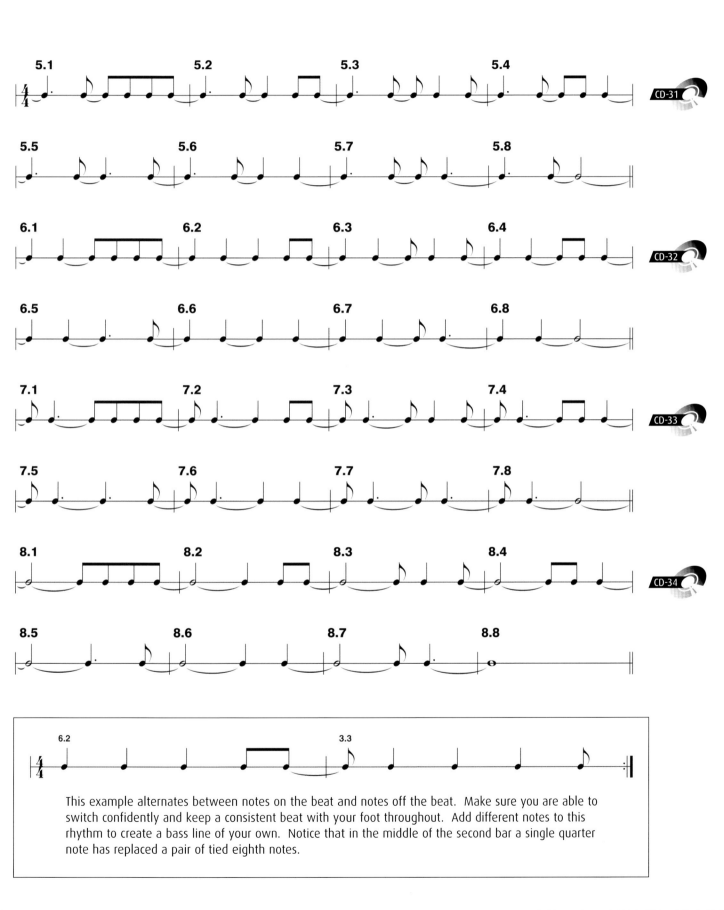

This example alternates between notes on the beat and notes off the beat. Make sure you are able to switch confidently and keep a consistent beat with your foot throughout. Add different notes to this rhythm to create a bass line of your own. Notice that in the middle of the second bar a single quarter note has replaced a pair of tied eighth notes.

key signatures

All major scales follow the same sequence of tones (T) and semitones (s). Each scale can be divided into two parts with each half consisting of the same pattern - T T s. Therefore the second half of a C scale - G A B C - is the first half of a G scale. The second half of the G scale, however, requires F♯ to put the final semitone in the correct place - D E F♯ G. This process can be repeated starting successive scales on the fifth note of the previous one, each time sharpening the seventh note to maintain the correct tone/semitone sequence:

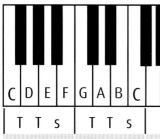

											SHARPS
1	2	3	4	5	6	7	8				
C	D	E	F	G	A	B	C				0
		G	A	B	C	D	E	F♯	G		1
			D	E	F♯	G	A	B	C♯	D	2
				A	B	C♯	D	E	F♯	G♯ A	3
					E	F♯	G♯	A	B	C♯ D♯ E	4
						B	C♯	D♯	E	F♯ G♯ A♯ B	5
							F♯	G♯	A♯	B C♯ D♯ E♯ F♯	6

Reversing the process produces the flat keys. The first half of a C scale forms the second half of an F scale - which requires Bb to put the first semitone in the correct place. Repeating this involves flattening the fourth note each time:

											FLATS
						1	2	3	4	5 6 7 8	
						C	D	E	F	G A B C	0
					F G A Bb	C	D	E	F		1
				Bb C D Eb	F	G	A	Bb			2
			Eb F G Ab	Bb	C	D	Eb				3
		Ab Bb C Db	Eb	F	G	Ab					4
	Db Eb F Gb	Ab	Bb	C	Db						5
Gb Ab Bb Cb	Db	Eb	F	Gb							6

Notice that:

• Every scale follows the musical alphabet.

• Sharps and flats do not occur in the same scale.

• The last sharp in a key signature is the seventh note of the scale.

• The last flat in a key signature is the fourth note of the scale.

• The number of sharps corresponds to the open strings –
  G 1, D 2, A 3, E 4.

• The number of flats corresponds to the first fret in the opposite direction –
  F 1, Bb 2, Eb 3, Ab 4.

The following diagram includes all the previous information and shows:

• The relative minor of each major key.

• The primary chords in each key, since the cycle is in fifths clockwise and fourths anticlockwise:
  Key of Eb: Eb(I), Ab(IV), and Bb(V).

• The secondary chords in each key:
  Key of Eb: Cm (VI), Fm (II), Gm (III).

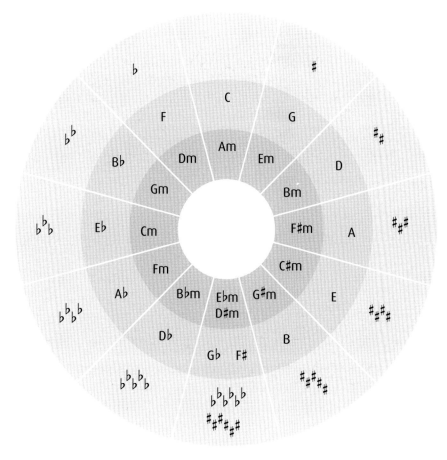

Seventh chords based on thirds use alternate letters from the musical alphabet - with sharps or flats as necessary - so only the following "spellings" are possible:

R	3	5	7
A	C	E	G
B	D	F	A
C	E	G	B
D	F	A	C
E	G	B	D
F	A	C	E
G	B	D	F

This works for major seventh, dominant seventh, minor seventh, half-diminished and diminished seventh chords. For example:

	CHORD	KEY	R	3	5	7
II	B⌀	Am	B	D	F	A
V	B7	E	B	D♯	F♯	A
V	B♭7	E♭	B♭	D	F	A♭
VII	B°7	Cm	B	D	F	A♭

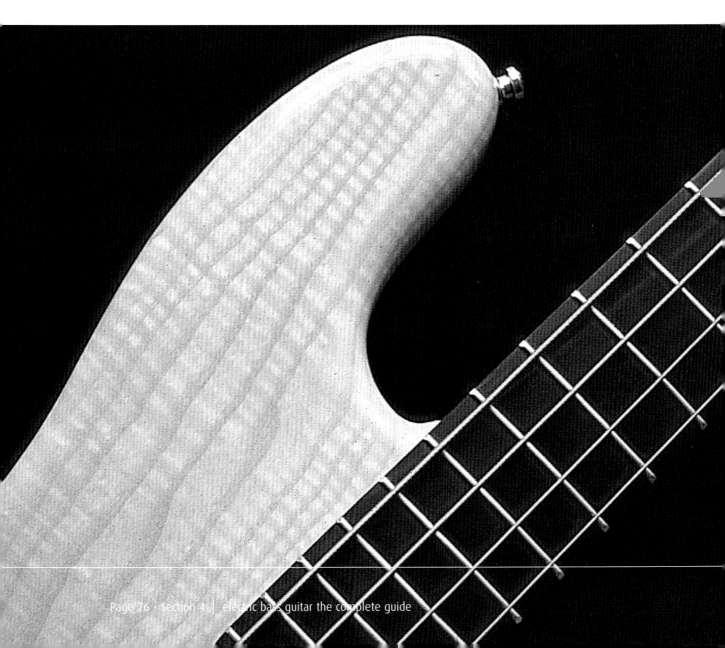

examples

When you have played all the complete bars, with and without ties, move on to the examples that follow. Initially, establish the rhythm before adding the notes. If necessary refer back to the stave layout, but don't write out the notes. It may seem quicker at first, but it won't encourage you to remember where they are on the stave.

Check that you are playing in the right octave.

Don't try to remember the separate sharps or flats from the key signature - just play the notes from the scale and alter it as required when accidentals occur - sharps (♯), flats (♭) and naturals (♮) which are effective until the end of the bar, unless cancelled by another accidental.

Reading music depends on recognising note and rhythm patterns. To develop this skill look at the music, and not at your fingers. When a series of notes occurs on consecutive lines and spaces it is a section of the scale - in this case decending a D scale from G down to D.

A sequence of adjacent lines or spaces means thirds - notes from a chord:

In each case just read the first note - you should know what the others will be.

As you complete each example check that you understand the connection between the bass notes and the chords. Also, consider any alternative position for the notes and whether your fingering could be improved. Usually it is better to use one position that contains all the notes and so avoid unnecessary shifts. If there is a choice, then the lowest position will give the clearest sound.

At the beginning of each piece, above the clef, the number of beats per minute is indicated. This can be set on a drum machine or a metronome, or used as a guide - 120 represents two beats per second.

On the CD each track starts with a hi-hat "count" followed by drums with guitar/keyboards.
Then the sequence is repeated with bass added.

Play this example in second position using all four fingers and no open strings. It can also be played with each note doubled:

Now play the same line in octaves starting at 12A. Play in as low a position as possible - use the A and G strings rather than the E and D. Initially ignore the slides (⟋) and then, when you do include them, don't change the rhythm. To keep time when playing a slide, start slowly and accelerate to arrive at the 'target' note exactly on the beat. When the slides are accurate play open A as you reach the top note.

In the next example the first notes of the groups form a G scale. This links the chords, emphasises their differences, and involves inversion where indicated. The suggested fingering allows a smooth change of position at the end of the second bar.

Play these lines in position, using the indicated fingering:

Now combine both lines to produce this exercise:

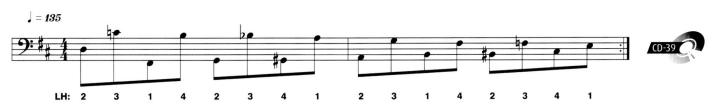

The notes on the E-string can be picked with the thumb.

A line over or under a note means that it should be held for its full length and not cut – because often, rather than notating every rest, the exact duration of notes is left to the player.

A dot over or under a note indicates that it is played staccato - cut short rather than sustained. Control the duration of each open E with your right-hand thumb.

In the following examples ties create the effect of anticipation - notes played before the beat rather than on it.

Notice that the third and fourth fingers are used on the same fret.

In this example the bass emphasises the difference between the chords. A tie over a bar line continues the effect of an accidental to the following note.

This line features sixths:

The next example is in C minor and includes G7 as the dominant chord (V) resolving to the tonic (I). F7 functions as a secondary dominant leading to B♭7.

This example is also in C minor. The seventh notes of the chords link the roots. This creates a line that is a descending scale. The B°7 (VII) leads back to Cm (I) and is an alternative to G7 (V), sharing its dominant function.

The next line has roots, thirds and fifths in octaves. 'Sim' indicates that the line is continued in a similar style while following the 12-bar sequence with the familiar I IV V chords.

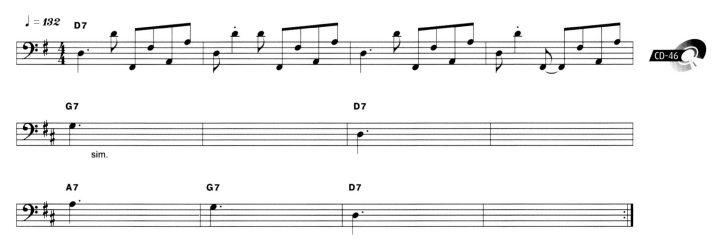

The following examples start on an 'up' - the eighth note before the bar line - beginning with a line built around the notes C♯ and E. These notes fit both chords - II and I in E. The bass line also implies chromatic passing chords - shown in brackets - illustrating the use of diminished seventh chords.

In the next example the chords are II/V and V in the key of D - subdominant and dominant. Notes marked 8va are played an octave higher than written. The low notes are played open.

Don't be confused by rests. For instance these rhythms are the same, but with notes either sustained, with ties and dots, or cut with rests:

Even though the augmented fourth in this example is not in the scale, it fits the chord better than the unaltered fourth - which would clash with the third, and disturb the chord's tonic function.

The following line features the five-note major pattern:

When a phrase can be played using only three frets then, unless in a high position, the fourth finger is used instead of the third.

The next example features the five-note minor pattern and has sections with contrasting rhythms:

The chords in brackets are not part of the basic sequence but are implied by the bass line. They create more movement and stronger changes. The rhythmic figure in the last two bars begins with four notes of equal length - effectively dotted quarter notes - which are alternately on and off the beat. Notice that in the first four bars the notes are cut, but in the last four they're sustained.

Also notice how inversions (F7/A, G7/B and A7/C♯) produce an ascending chromatic bass line which leads strongly back to the Dm7 chord. Inversion can also create a pedal note – where the bass repeats the same note while the chords change, for example – C F/C C. This generates tension which is released when the bass note finally changes. Inversion often occurs when the bass line follows a scale such as the example on page 79. Another possibility is when inversion produces repetition. In the following sequence the G7/B maintains the sequence of fourths in the bass –

C   F   G7/B   Em7   Am7   Dm7   G7

The following examples have rests at the beginning of bars. The effect is similar to that of a tie over the bar line, but the previous note is cut instead of being sustained:

In this line a simple root/sixth/fifth pattern is varied by adding octaves and then by inverting it on the D chord, to avoid high notes. The slight change of rhythm in the second and fourth bars extends and adds interest. Notice which notes are sustained and which are cut.

This example consists of a two-bar phrase extended to four bars by adding a different ending - so the second phrase 'answers' the first. This line can be played an octave lower.

The next example repeats three-note descending phrases. When notes of different pitch are joined by a slur, ⌢ or ⌣, only the first is picked. The other note is produced either by hammering on with another finger, or by sliding the finger to another fret while sustaining the sound.

This sequence is a minor blues. There is rhythmic contrast between the initial off-beat phrase and more on-beat patterns from the fifth bar:

This line can be played in position - all the notes are from the A scale. Inversion and varying rhythmic patterns create an effective line.

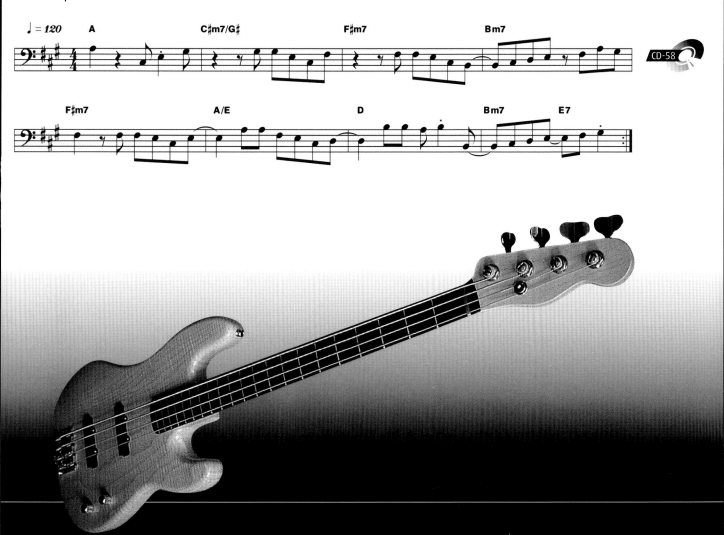

The following examples illustrate the musical ideas that can form the basis for the development of a bass line. The basic dotted rhythm is maintained and the chord sequence is the classic "turnaround"– I VI IV V or I VI II V.

Initially play just root notes –

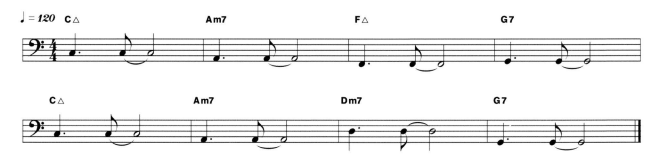

Scale notes link the roots and also relate to the respective chords – so the B linking C to A is the major seventh of the C chord. Alternatively these notes can also imply the additional bracketed chords.

In this version the connecting note is also the fifth of the next chord –

Now combine the two previous lines –

This time the last note in each bar is semitone below the next root. Where this is a chromatic note it may imply the secondary dominant indicated.

(E7)   **(D7)**

Combining all the previous lines -

Introducing more ideas with more chromatic links and more rhythmic variations –

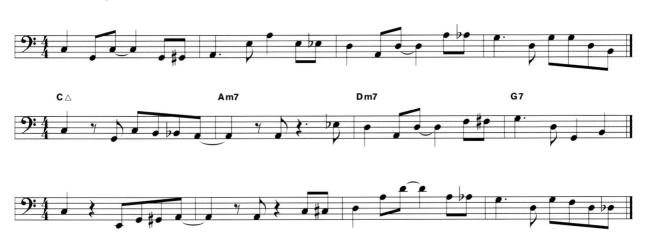

These "demonstration" lines have been developed in a deliberate step-by-step process. However, once the musical effect of these ideas has been absorbed, lines like these will occur in response to the requirements of the music and the input of the other musicians.

Now a chromatic exercise which can be played entirely on the G string using the indicated fingering:

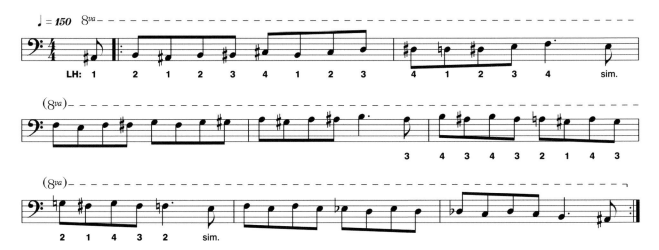

The remaining examples in this section feature sixteenth notes. As with eighth note divisions of a half note, there are only eight patterns based on sixteenth note divisions of a quarter note:

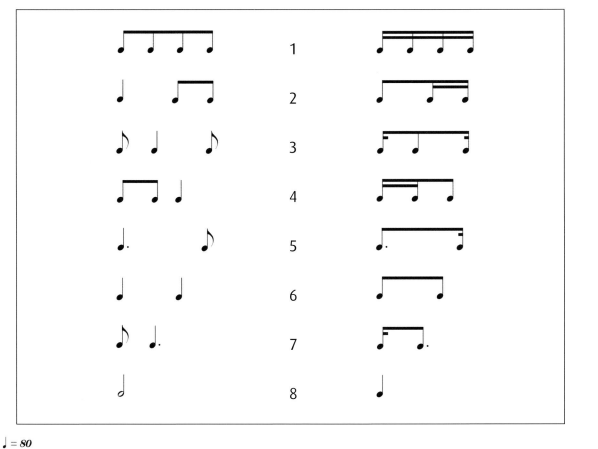

Initially the pairs of sixteenth notes can be replaced by single eighth notes to establish the basic rhythm:

The following example features octaves and sixteenth notes. The correct sequence of right-hand fingering is essential, so initially practise slowly. For the E-string the thumb can be used instead of the first finger.

RH: 1   1 2 Th   1 2 Th   1 2 Th   1 2   1   2   1   2   1   1

The next example has a blues feel - with the minor third and augmented fourth adding extra tension. Notice how the original two-bar phrase is repeated with variations - an anticipation and a different ending. The second bar features repetition of similar intervals - D>G#, C#>G and B>F# - which gives shape to the line. The slurs in the first and third bars are produced by hammering on, and those in the last bar with slides.

Now a line built around the five-note minor pattern, with some chromatic links:

If the rests are confusing then remember that with sustained notes the same rhythm would be written:

The next example introduces a dotted rhythm - in this case it involves playing a quick note just before the second beat. Tap the rhythm first to make sure it's correct.

Now another example featuring the five-note major pattern:

The opening rhythmic phrase in the next exercise is one that must be recognised at sight. Start by tapping it - initially without the tie. There are chromatic links to each new root. These become one note longer each time. Position these notes in relation to the next beat - not by calculating the duration of the rests.

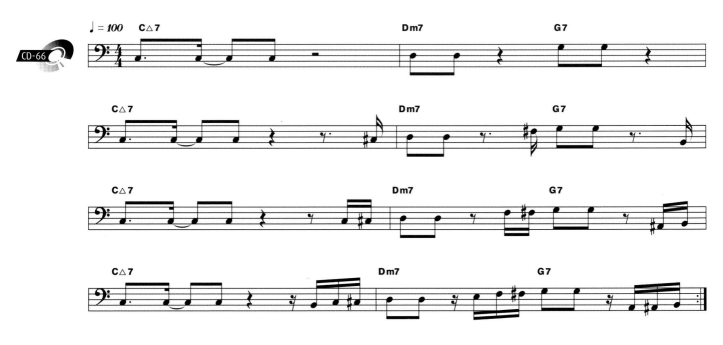

The following example has groups containing four sixteenth notes. Every note must be clear. The last group in the fourth and eighth bars involves one note on the beat and another - which is accented (>) - immediately after the beat. This is equivalent to playing the first two of a group of four sixteenth notes.

The last two bars illustrate an alternative use of inversion - pedal point. The bass line repeats G, while the chords change from Cm7 to G7.

The next example includes all the intervals of a fifth associated with a major chord:
root > fifth > ninth/second > sixth > tenth/third.

The following lines have:
- Dead notes (♩) - notes played while the left hand mutes the string.

- Grace notes (♪) - notes which take their time from the note they are tied to. They are kept as short as possible.

In the next line inversion produces semitone steps:

This example is mainly roots and fifths but the rhythm is varied to add interest. It also includes a new pattern.

The next examples feature similar notes - again the minor third with the dominant seventh chord.

Now a line based on the semitone/tone diminished scale. This includes the notes of the dominant seventh chord but adds a minor second (♭9), minor third (♭10) and augmented fourth (♯11).

The following piece, in A minor - although it strays into A major - is built on a rhythmic figure, repeated with variations. Tap out the rhythm first, initially replacing the rests with notes and omitting the ties.

These lines can be played as a duet or by recording one and accompanying yourself. The melody relates to Dm7 - the upper part of G11.

Now a line which follows a familiar sequence - I, VI, II, V. Various ascending and descending runs are used with different rhythms. The last note on the G7 is just after the fourth beat:

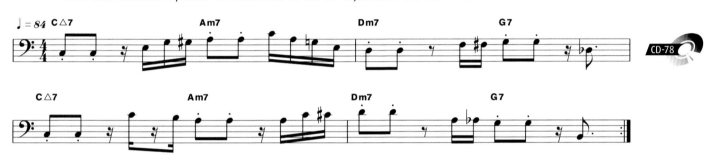

The interval of a fourth creates interesting lines - with C or Am the notes E, A, D, G, C.
The next example features fourths around A7:

reading music

The following examples involve playing more continuous sixteenth notes.

This last example has a semitone step at the start of each bar. On A7 it leads to the third, and on D7 to the root. Rhythmic patterns are repeated, but with variations in the second and fourth bars. There are more semitone steps on the D7 - first to the minor third (♭10) and then to the major third.

triplet rhythms

In the previous sections the rhythms have been based on a quarter-note beat divided into two eighth notes, or four sixteenth notes. In this section the beat is divided into three. This creates a problem, however, since notation is based on halving notes to produce shorter ones. One solution is to indicate that three notes are played in the time of two. This is written:

Practise this rhythm, making sure the triplets are even. The alternative way to write this is to use a dotted quarter-note beat which can then be divided into three eighth notes:

Although writing in $\frac{12}{8}$ avoids having to indicate triplets, $\frac{4}{4}$ is more usual.

Now play only the first and third note of each triplet:

Alternate this with bars of triplets to make sure the rhythm is correct - it should sound familiar. In practice ♩ ♪ is usually written ⌐ or even ⌐ , so:

Would be written:

or:

So when ♩. ♩ occurs with triplets it's interpreted as ♩ ♪. Notice that with triplets the dotted rhythms are in half-note groups, whereas for sixteenth notes they would be in quarter-note groups.

The next two bars are almost the same, except that in the second bar the last note of the triplet is omitted:

This includes the four basic triplet rhythm patterns. Now add ties:

The end of the second bar now involves playing three equal notes over two beats. It would be written:

The first exercise is written in ⁶⁄₈ - two beats to the bar, with a triplet division. The middle note of each group is A, and the outside notes are always octaves. Follow the fingering shown and aim initially for an accurate flowing rhythm rather than speed.

Now a line built around the familiar I, VI, II, V sequence. The initial instruction ♫ = ♩ ♪ indicates a triplet feel and means that the final ♪ ♩ ♪ is played as ♩ ♪ ♩ ♪. Every low A is played open. Notice the flattened fifth in the last bar. The bracketed tie is only played on the repeat.

In the next two examples the dotted eighth rest produces the same rhythm as a tie on to a dotted eighth note.

The next line features descending chromatic notes and a double dotted note. Each dot adds half the value of the previous one. This means that ♩.. ♪ equals ♩ 𝅘𝅥𝅮

The following examples are both written with an instruction to interpret the even eighth notes as a triplet rhythm:

Only the first note of the last four is picked - the G is hammered on, then a pull off for the F and a hammer on the fifth fret from open A for the D.

The triplet in the last bar of the next line includes a double sharp – F✕ equivalent to G♮. This reduces the number of accidentals. Apart from this note the whole line is within the scale of A and can be played in position. The first four bars are repeated as indicated. The last four bars feature a repeated pattern - but varied to fit the scale - where the roots and fifths are played by laying the first finger across both strings and shifting pressure from one to the other.

The next line is built around a G7 chord with the ♭10 (minor third) and #11 (augmented fourth) creating a bluesy sound:

The next two examples may be easier to read in $\frac{2}{2}$ - two half-note beats per bar. The first example is based on a rhythmic phrase, repeated with variations, and interval patterns - the root/fifth/ninth sequence and semitone runs from ninth to octave or from ninth to tenth. Keep these ideas in mind when continuing the line through the other chords:

Now a VI, II, V, I progression with an implied secondary dominant on III to resolve to the VI chord. Notice how flattened fifths lead to the root of each new chord as the sequence moves in fourths. Make sure that you distinguish between notes that are sustained and those that are cut.

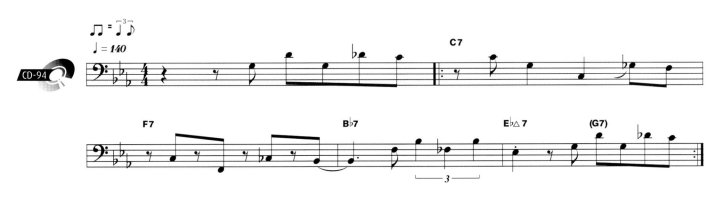

The next example is a 12-bar blues sequence with the bass line featuring tritones.

In bars 9 and 10 complex chords are created from simple elements –
A/G = G13^{+11}
B♭/A♭ = A♭13^{+11}
G7/C♯ = C♯7^{b5b9} (or C♯7^{alt})

The final examples both feature sixteenth-note triplets. Initially reading may be easier with an eighth-note beat. The relationship between the beat and the bass line is then the same as in the previous examples. As soon as the rhythm is accurate return to a quarter-note beat.

Every A is played open.

electric bass guitar | section five

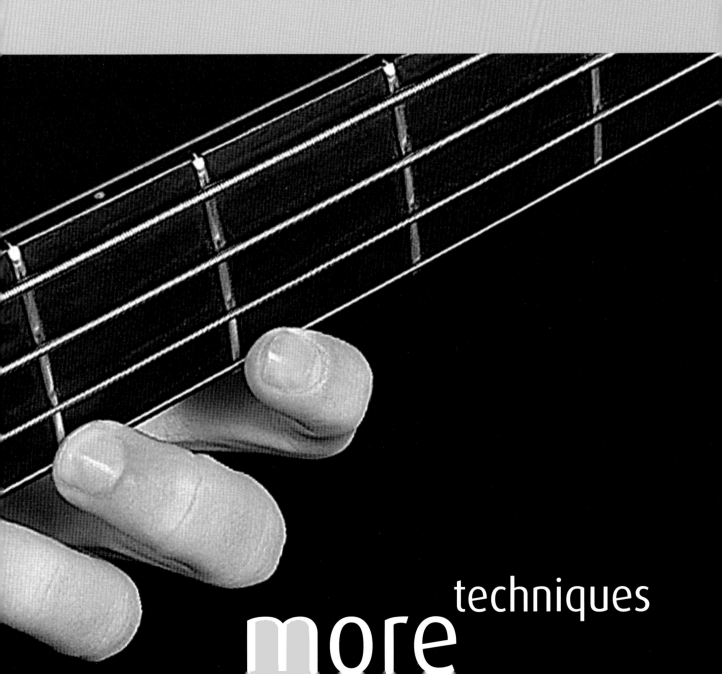

more techniques

walking bass

This section is a sequence of exercises designed to build the musical skills required to create walking bass lines to given chord sequences. The ability to do this will also help the development of other types of bass line.

The focus will be on note choice, with the rhythm kept simple. Begin by playing a two-in-a-bar line with just roots and fifths –

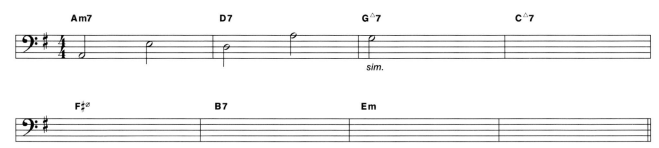

This sounds repetitive, and does not "walk". The line is improved if the fifths are played alternately above and below the roots –

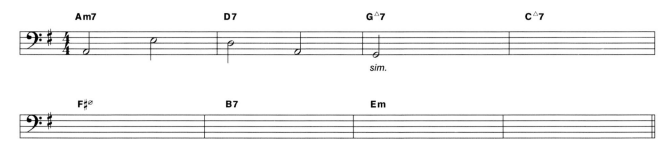

Now substitute thirds (above or below) for the fifths. Notice how a third leads up to the next root when a sequence moves in fourths..

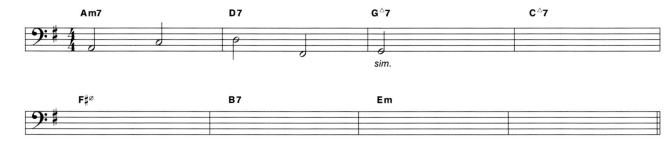

Finally, you should be able to mix and vary the basic chord notes -

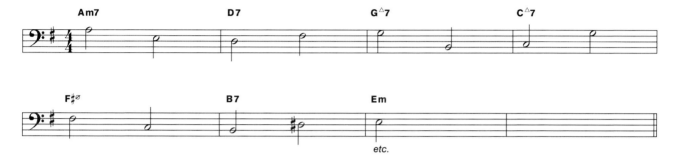

So far this should be straightforward, and you should be able to do this confidently at sight with any chord sequence. If necessary revise the section on seventh chords (**2.4**). Now play root/third/fifth/seventh on each chord in turn. Again, this sounds more like an exercise than a walking line –

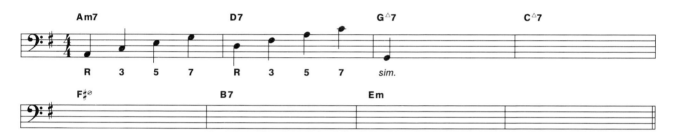

Next, still playing only chord notes, at each chord change move to the nearest note in the next chord –

Generally the root is played on the chord change – to make that change clear. Alternatively, a chord note which still makes the chord's function clear and distinguishes it from the previous chord – an exception is when the bass note is a pedal.

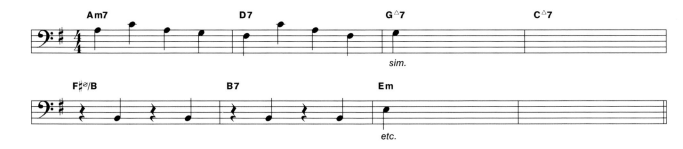

Finally, add scale notes and other chromatic notes. It's important to realise that although the sequence starts on Am7, it is not in the key of A minor. It begins with II V I IV in G major and finishes with II V I in E minor (see **3.3**).

Chromatic steps help to produce a characteristic walking line and create more tension and urgency – often bass players will alter notes chromatically to generate this effect, as in this line based on the I (or III) VI II V "turn-around" sequence – see chord function (**3.2**). There are also secondary dominants (**3.4**) and chord substitutions (**3.5**). Fluency with these concepts will enable you to create effective lines. The section on Bach's Cello Suites (**5.5**) will help develop the technique required to play those lines confidently.

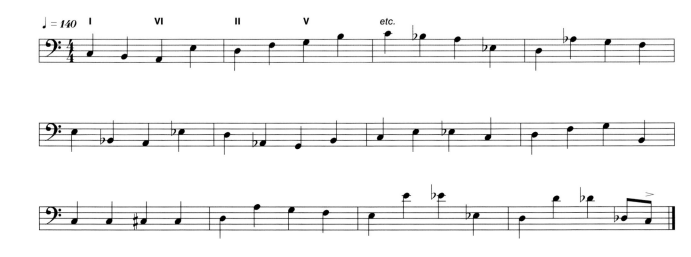

chording

This involves playing two or more notes together. It will usually sound better:
• With large intervals - tenths rather than thirds, for example.
• In high positions.
• Using the back pickup - which produces a clearer tone.

Tenths are simply thirds played an octave higher. These can be played separately or together, ascending and descending the scale. The tenths occur as major or minor in exactly the same scale positions as for thirds. As the interval is much larger, start by playing a G scale entirely on the E-string and then add the appropriate tenths on the G-string.

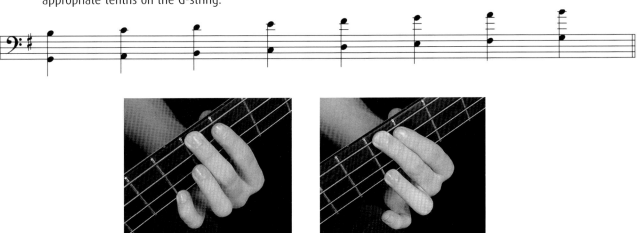

This example includes the possible tenths for a dominant seventh chord, with parallel chromatic links. The fourth does not occur, as it would disturb the function of the chord.

The next examples have the same chords with tenths either played together or separately in a standard major key sequence:

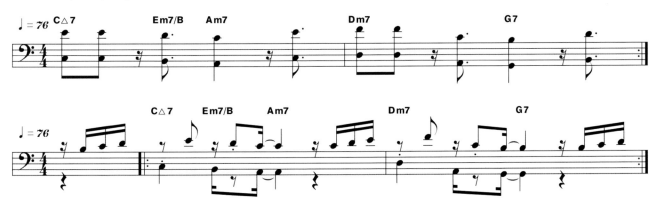

more techniques

This example has various combinations - tenths, sevenths and an eleventh - in a typical minor key sequence:

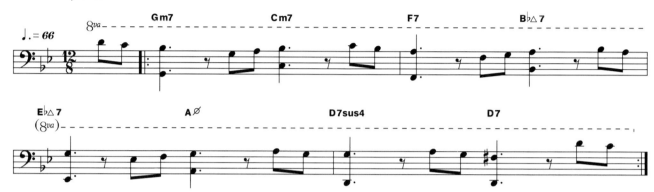

The pairs of notes in the next examples are the third and seventh of each chord.

When dominant seventh chords move in a sequence of fourths, their thirds and sevenths fall in semitones, to sevenths and thirds respectively.

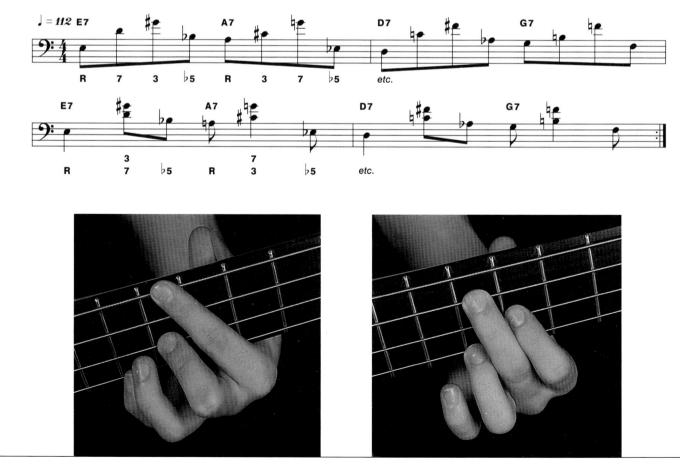

In the following example there are chromatic runs up to thirds and down to sevenths, each with a different rhythm. The roots and fifths are played on open strings. Begin by tapping the rhythm of the two parts combined.

Next, a 12-bar sequence with tenths played as separate notes. Notice how the fingering changes for different positions.

The brace indicates that the notes on both staves are played together on one instrument.

The notes on the lower stave are played open with the E-string tuned down to D.

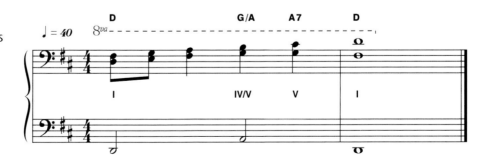

harmonics

Every note on the bass consists of a series of related harmonics. Natural harmonics are produced from an open string. Sustain an open note and then touch the string to produce these harmonics. This reveals their presence in the original note. The first harmonic is the lowest and is heard as the note's pitch. The others reinforce it and add tonal colour. To emphasise the first harmonic, pick the open string at its mid-point - the twelfth fret.

The second harmonic is produced by touching the string at its mid-point. This mutes the first harmonic, but allows the second and other even-numbered harmonics to sound. As the second harmonic does not vibrate at the mid-point it, and all even-numbered harmonics, are absent if the string is picked at that point. Confirm this by picking at the twelfth fret and then immediately touching the string at the same point - no harmonic will sound. So, if it is ever necessary to mute a note with your right hand, touch the string at the point where you picked to minimise unwanted harmonics.

Picking closer to the bridge encourages higher harmonics relative to lower ones, and so produces a brighter tone. Similarly, the back (bridge) pickup has a brighter sound than the front one because it receives a greater proportion of higher harmonics.

The third harmonic is produced by touching the string a third of the way along - either over the seventh or nineteenth fret. Using both hands, it is possible to touch the string at both points without muting the harmonic - provided that it is not touched elsewhere.

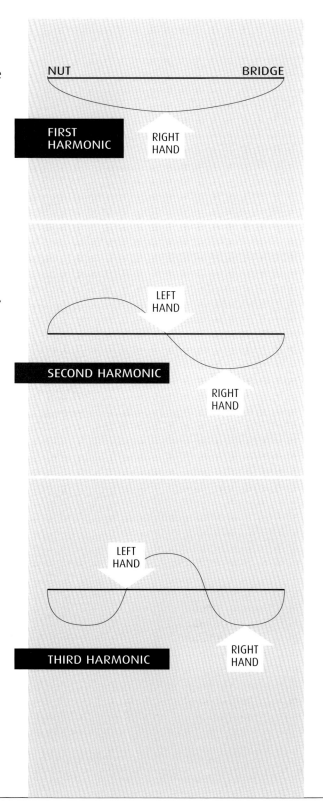

Harmonics can be notated in two ways:
• By indicating the pitch in the normal way and placing a small circle above the note. So H12A is written:

With this system the treble (G) clef is required for the higher notes. The treble stave continues up from the bass stave:

This is the same as:

• By indicating where the harmonic is found. So H12A is written:

The lower note represents the string to be played and the upper diamond-shaped symbol the position where the string is touched. This method has two advantages:
• The harmonics can be written on the bass stave.
• It indicates exactly where the harmonic is found. This is helpful, especially when there is a choice of position.

The disadvantage of this method is that certain harmonics - the sixth, seventh and eighth - do not coincide with a fret position:

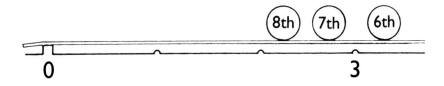

This chart shows the natural harmonics on all strings, using both systems:

- Every halving of the string produces an octave – the first, second, fourth and eighth harmonics are a series of octave steps. The third and sixth harmonics are also an octave apart.

- Seventh harmonics are very flat - about 30% of a semitone - and this restricts their use.

- Fifth harmonics are slightly flat - about 10% of a semitone - and need to be used with care. This discrepancy occurs because a major third produced from a series of perfect fifths - G>D>A>E>B - is sharp compared with its true pitch, which corresponds to the fifth harmonic.

- Third harmonics are very slightly sharp. So, when the cycle of fifths returns to the original note, another discrepancy occurs. To eliminate this the fifths are slightly flattened - 'tempered' - to maintain perfect octaves. This produces equal semitones - 'equal temperament' - enabling:
  - All keys to be used.
  - Tritone substitution to be possible. For example, by making Db and C♯ equal, Eb7 may be substituted for A7 and vice-versa.

Harmonics do not conform to the semitone/fret system and so knowing where to find particular notes can be a problem. The simplest, and most musical, approach is to treat the harmonics of any string as the notes of a chord, with the open string as the root. The fourth to ninth harmonics on the G-string correspond to G9: G B D F G A. Exactly the same pattern occurs on the other strings.

Harmonics may be used to produce chords. Initially select a pair of harmonics on adjacent strings at the same fret - such as H5D and H5G, which produce the notes D and G respectively. These can be combined with different root notes:

Harmonics	G	G	G	G	G
	D	D	D	D	D
Fretted Note (root)	Eb	E	F	A	Bb
Chord	Eb△7	Em7	F6/9	A7sus4	Bb6

• Adjust the position of the left hand so that it only touches the string/s at the appropriate point/s. Play the notes separately to check that they are all sounding.
• Remove the finger/s from the string/s as soon as the harmonic/s sound.
• Pick the strings close to the bridge, using your thumb for the root and fingernails for the harmonics.
• If your bass is not fitted with a pickup near the bridge, some harmonics will not be heard.

Combine other pairs of harmonics with different root notes. Also consider non-adjacent combinations and groups of three or four harmonics. When forming chords the fifth is not important, unless it is diminished or augmented. If possible avoid duplicating notes.

In this example, when harmonics are repeated, only the rhythm has been shown:

In the following examples the harmonics are written on the treble stave.

The position of the root note determines where the harmonics are played. The final chord contains ninth harmonics that require accurate technique from both hands. This piece is not in C, but as it does not conform to any key it has been written with an 'open' key signature.

The volume control can be used to 'swell' harmonic chords. Start with the volume down, play the chord and then fade it in.

Artificial harmonics are produced from a fretted string, rather than an open one. They can be played in several ways:

• By touching the mid-point of the sounding section of string with the right-hand thumb and picking with the first fingernail. The harmonic is an octave above the fretted note:

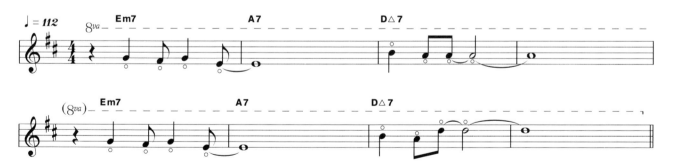

This technique works best on the top strings, above the twelfth fret. Move the right hand closer to the bridge - a quarter of the distance from bridge to fret – and the harmonic is two octaves above the fretted note.

• In lower positions, by fretting the string normally and, instead of picking, tapping it twelve frets higher. Again the harmonic is an octave above the fretted note.

If you disregard the 8va then the notes indicate the left-hand position.

• In high positions, by fretting the string with the first finger or thumb. The harmonic is produced by touching the string with another finger at the appropriate point - four, five or seven frets higher.

slapping

Before starting this section there are some basic points to consider:
- Although slapping is performed with the right hand, it involves left-hand technique to control the notes, mute the strings, hammer-on and pull-off.
- Your bass needs to be correctly adjusted with a low action - especially over the top frets - and lighter strings.
- All the examples can also be played with 'normal' technique – you may find it useful to do this first.

Begin by placing your hand in the position illustrated, with the side of your thumb lying parallel to the A-string near the end of the fingerboard. Now rotate your hand and forearm together, and flick your hand at the string, so that the side of the thumb - between the tip and first joint - hits the string. Then let your thumb bounce off, so that contact with the string is as brief as possible. Your hand should be loose and relaxed - the action is like shaking a wet hand dry. The slap is created by directing the weight of the hand at the string, and not by any deliberate action with the hand or thumb.

First slap a muted A string, touched at C but not fretted:

Now fret the string using the left hand to keep the notes short:

Octaves are added by pulling the G-string with the first finger and allowing it to snap against the frets. This action is not separate from the slap. The fingertip is hooked under the string and pulls it as the wrist rotates when the thumb bounces off. Again, begin with muted strings:

The roots and fifths are slapped and the octaves pulled:

Make sure that the triplet rhythm is accurate:

♩. = 120

In the next two examples each A is open:

♩ = 80

♩ = 120   Bm7

The dead notes have been bracketed, as they are not essential and can be confusing to read. You will probably play them anyway, as they help to maintain the rhythm and flow of your right hand.

Each open E is slapped with the thumb and kept short. The pairs of notes are produced by tapping the strings with the first and second fingers:

♩ = 120   Em7

♩ = 104   G   G7/B   C   A7   C/D   D7

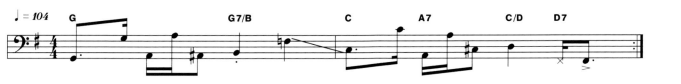

more techniques

This pattern is based on repeated intervals of a fifth. Notice how each triplet group occurs with both chords.

The ♭10 chord adds a blues feel:

The following example is played entirely with the thumb and involves hammering-on from muted open strings:

The next example includes a pair of thirty-second notes which, initially, may be replaced by a single sixteenth note.

The next example features semitone slides:

These lines involve hammering-on from open strings:

The final example is a complete 12-bar blues sequence:

Bach's cello suites

These pieces are very different from typical bass lines. However, they pose various technical problems and are excellent practice. The technical demands will help improve your playing generally.

This is the second minuet from the first suite. The second section consists of chord patterns. Awareness of the harmonic structure will suggest fingering and help you to remember the music. The chords are not always played from the root. Notice how half-diminished and diminished seventh patterns occur over dominant seventh chords - adding ninths, major and minor respectively:

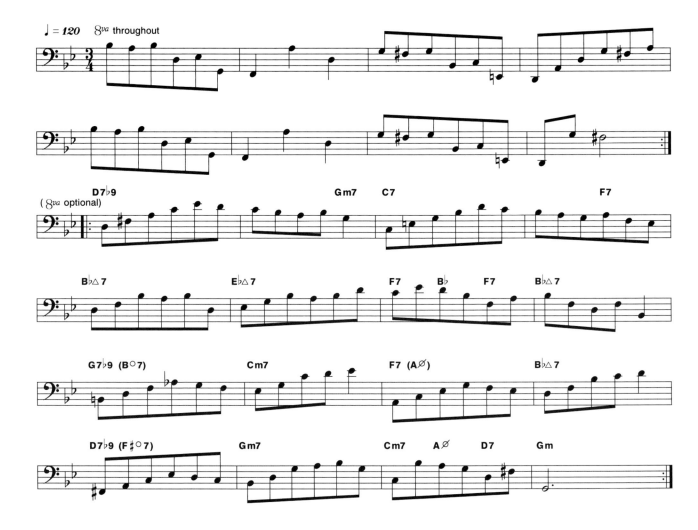

Next, an excerpt from the first gavotte of the sixth suite. Start by practising the chords and then add the other notes.

If your bass can reach an E – the 21st fret on the G-string – then you can also play it in G, producing brighter, clearer chords.

more techniques

Now, the courante from the first suite. Although its range is not great - the highest note is the E at 9G - the position shifts need some thought. The bars marked ☐ 1 are played the first time. The second time, after the repeat, play those marked ☐ 2

For the two-bar sections marked * use this fingering: 1421 2411 1414 | 1421 2413 1414
Although this involves more movement than strict position playing, it is faster and more relaxed.

Finally, the first bourree from the third suite. The opening section involves high positions and chords. This piece covers almost the whole range of the bass and so fingering requires careful planning - start with the chords, as each can only be played in one position. Initially divide the music into two or four bar phrases and, where possible, play each phrase in a single position. Then gradually assemble the sections until the piece is complete. Notice that phrases do not coincide with bars, and usually start with a pair of eighth notes before a bar line.

Tony BACON & Barry MOORHOUSE	**The Bass Book**	
Tony BACON & Gareth MORGAN	**Paul McCartney - Bassmaster**	
Karl CORYAT (ed)	**The Bass Player Book**	
John DeWITT	**Rhythmic Figures for Bassists**	(unavailable)
Dan DEAN	**Electric Bass Composite**	
Dan DEAN	**The Studio Bassist**	
Andy DOERSCHUK (ed)	**Electric Bass Guitar**	
Ed FRIEDLAND	**The Working Bassist's Tool Kit**	
John GOLDSBY	**The Jazz Bass Book**	
Barry GREEN	**The Inner Game of Music**	
Jonas HELLBORG	**Thumb Basics**	
Joe HUBBARD	**Basslines**	
Joe HUBBARD	**Pop Basslines**	
Jay HUNGERFORD	**Walking Jazz Lines for Bass**	
Carol KAYE	**Electric Bass Lines Complete 1&2**	
MAKING MUSIC	**What Bass**	
Bill MILKOWSKY	**Jaco**	

Tom MULHERN (ed)	Bass Heroes	
Adam NOVICK	Harmonics for Electric Bass	
Tony OPPENHEIM	Slap It!	
Jaco PASTORIUS	Modern Electric Bass	(DVD)
John PATITUCCI	Electric Bass	(DVD)
Rufus REID	The Evolving Bassist	
Mike RICHMOND	Modern Walking Bass Technique	
Jim ROBERTS	How the Fender Bass Changed the World	
Keith ROSIER	Studio Bass Masters	
Chuck SHER	The Improviser's Bass Method	
Allan "Dr Licks" SLUTSKY	Funkmasters - The Great James Brown Rhythm Sections	
Allan "Dr Licks" SLUTSKY	Standing in the Shadows of Motown	
	- The Life and Music of Legendary Bassist James Jamerson	
Allan "Dr Licks" SLUTSKY	Standing in the Shadows of Motown	(DVD)
Paul WESTWOOD	Bass Bible	
Paul WESTWOOD	The Complete Bass Guitar Player	(DVD)

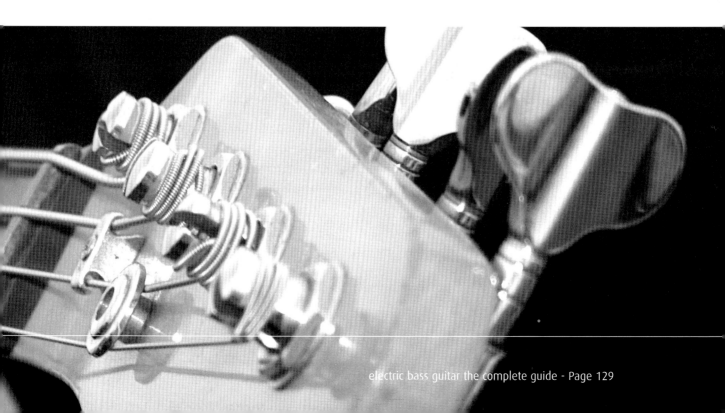

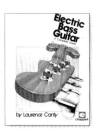

Electric Bass Guitar – a complete guide
59 pages

I had started giving private lessons in 1974 and soon had the idea of writing a book. Then, in December 1975, Stuart McGowan – a guitarist I had played with at Lancaster University - mentioned that Chappells were interested in publishing a bass tutor. In a meeting in February 1976 meeting they revealed that they might translate a French tutor they already published. However, in July, they decided to proceed with my book, and the contract was signed.

The original draft was hand-written in a week during an August break in Lancaster. It was typed and delivered on time at the beginning of October – just as I was starting to teach bass at Goldsmith's College, University of London – the class had been started by Mo Foster the previous year. There was then a long delay before it was published in December 1978 – although this did allow for various additions, with the basic rhythm patterns being included at the last moment.

The book was entirely designed and illustrated by John Stoddard. Its modern look was very different from other music books of the time.

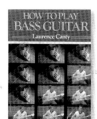

How to Play Bass Guitar
98 pages

Chappells had merged with EMI to become IMP. In 1983 IMP and Elm Tree Book wanted a bass book as part of a "How to" series. This provided an opportunity to revise and make additions. The work was typed during a summer season on the Isle of Man and published in 1984. It also appeared in French and Spanish translations.

Electric Bass Guitar – the complete guide
95 pages

I suggested to IMP that it was time for a new revised, improved, enlarged edition and this emerged in 1990. The previous text was typed into a word processor and then the changes were made. The new material was inspired by the variety of freelance playing I had been involved in. This formed the basis of my teaching, especially for the classes at Goldsmith's College - where I continued to teach until 1997 – which required that this information was presented as clearly and simply as possible.

Electric Bass Guitar - the complete guide
130 pages

Once the previous version was out of print I was able to regain my copyright. So in 2009, over 30 years on from the original publication, and back in Lancaster, a new version is published. Now the whole process is computerised - from the writing to design and printing. The original drawings (which were created from photos) have been replaced by photos.

A consistent feature has been the bass on the front cover. When built in 1976 by John Diggins (of John Birch Guitars) it was all maple. On the latest cover it now has an ash body and ebony fingerboard – both by Dave Wild (of Wild Guitars, London).